How to Re
Story That is Ove

*Secrets of Regaining Love in a
Relationship and Improving Lost
Feelings*

Table of Contents

Chapter 1

Introduction

Love is defined as a complex set of emotions, conduct and convictions linked to strong affection, protection, warmth and respect for another person. Life can also be used for animals, values, and religious beliefs which are not human. For instance, a person could say that he or she loves his dog and loves liberty or God.

Since centuries love has been a favorite theme in which thinkers, poets, authors and scholars have often struggled to describe love. Although the majority agree that love means a strong feeling of affection, there are many differences about its exact meaning and that the "I Love You" of one person may mean something very different. Other possible love meanings include: a willingness to give priority to the well-being or happiness of others above yourself.

- Strong feelings of love, need and connection.
- Dramatic, unexpected sexy, respectful feeling.
- A passing love, concern, and common feeling.

The ability to support, respect and look after others, for example in marriage or when you have a son.

Some of the above feelings mixed.

There has been considerable debate about if love is an option, something lasting or passing and about the biological conditioning or social incoherence of love between family members and spouses.

Relationship can differ between individual and person and culture. In some time and place, each of the conversations about love may be exact. For example, love can be a choice in some instances, while love can feel uncontrollable in others.

It can be difficult to tell the difference between love and lust especially at the early stages of the relationship. Both of these are related to the physical attractiveness and an intoxicating rush of fresh chemicals, along with the often intense desire to come closer to someone else.

Love is something developed between two people and evolves over time, through getting to know him and the whole of life. Engagement, money, mutual trust and acceptance are involved.

On the other hand, desire has to do with the sensations driven by sex, which initially draw people into one another. Characterized by sex hormones and idealistic enthusiasm, lust blurs our ability to see an individual for whom it is and thus may or may not lead to a long-term relationship.

Some could claim that the perfect intimate relationship is a healthy mixture of love and desire. Lust for someone is typically an important early part of a longer-term partnership, and it is a worth cultivating practice for committed couples to revive the initial spark.

Everyone can agree that love plays an important role both in physical and emotional well-being, although almost no one can agree on the definition of love. Many studies have shown love's advantages. The role of love in mental health is far-reaching, however: the fact that babies without regular rearing or cuddling are delayed or sick in development can include some examples. Living with love in mental health

Feeling unloved is strongly related to low self-esteem and depression sensations.

People who both feel loved and report loving others tend to be happier.

Love can play a part in long-term health. Emotionally connected feelings can contribute to increasing immunity.

What is a love relationship?

There are many things in a relationship–friendship, sexual attraction, intellectual compatibility and, naturally, love. Love is the bond that has a strong and solid partnership. But if you really are in love, how do you know? These are some signs of a happy, life-enhancing passion for the emotion you experience.

1. Notwithstanding the phrase "at first sight, it was love," love does not feel immediately. Like a magnet dragging you into the person you just met, this strong feeling of attraction? This is sexual chemistry and infatuation. Mother Nature offers us a huge amount of enthusiasm to initially bind us together. Love includes sex chemistry, but it differs because it takes time to build an emotion. Lust can appear in an instant; Love develops in and out of the other person over a period of time.

2. A relationship without love is not really a full-faceted relationship, but that doesn't mean you like your partner immensely and sexually. When the romantic spark comes down, you will get lonely if you haven't built a basis for loving feelings with your partner.

3. Love takes time to flourish, like good wine, Love relationships are not established within a day. Love's threads take a long time to form a strong bond with each other. Only by shaving your feelings, cravings, dreams and hopes with you and your partner can love come into being. Therefore don't hurry love and trust the system. It has its own timetable, which must not be rushed and valued.

4. Is just one true love there?

We speak of "soul mates," but people are built to love more and more and over and over again. We would never recover from the loss of the spouse to divorce or death or forget our high school crush otherwise.

5. Love is generous: We give to the other without expecting a return in a truly loving relationship. We don't tell who did what for the other person. Pleasure is also a pleasure for our partner.

6. When we see our partner happy, we always get a feeling of happiness. We sense their blue mood when we see that they're sad or depressed. Love brings empathy for the emotional state of another person.

7. If we like someone, we are willing to compromise in order to respond to their needs or desires. Love means compromise. But in so doing, we don't risk our own selves or the others will ask us to sacrifice our own selves. This is not love; control and abuse. That's not love.

8. We value each other and love each other. We care for each other. Our partner is not deliberately harmed or degraded. It is with such calmness that the listeners can hear love in our voices as they talk about them in their absence. We are not behind their backs criticizing our partner.

9. Our love of the other person allows us to behave with them and in our society socially, morally and ethically. Their presence in our lives makes us want to be a better person, to keep admiring us.

10. In love, we never feel alone, even when isolated. We are protectors of one another's solitude. The other person's very thought gives us the feeling that we always have a guardian angel with us.

11. When our partner succeeds in something after a long time, we are joyful like winners too. Their winds are sources of happiness for us, not jealousy. There is no joy or competition, it is only a pleasure to see the success of our loved one.

12. They will always be in the minds of us even if our thoughts are separate from one another for work, travelling or other obligations and what they can do' right now.'

13. In passion, sex is sacred. Physical intimacy deepens. Unlike in the beginning, our love is now intense and sacred, a real union of bodies and minds.

14. This helps us to feel safe and secure in our marriage, as if another person is a safe haven to come to our house. We feel a sense of safety and stability with them.

15. Our partner knows us for who we are and still loves us. We feel seen and heard. We should reveal our positive and negative sides and unconditionally embrace their affection. You know who our heart is. Love enables us to bare our souls and in return feel grace.

16. In our love relationship, secure, we know we could argue and not break us apart. Love enables us to struggle without fear. We agree to disagree, and for too long we have no grudges, because it is not our partner's good to have a bad feeling.

Chapter 2

Qualities of a Good Man

Being a good person can seem like a complicated endeavor in modern society in today's fast-paced world, but it is actually not that hard to do. It requires an unwavering determination to comply with your internal code of honor. In the end, you must exemplify the following features in order to be an extraordinary symbol of manhood. Such qualities reflect the good nature of a man directly. Self-determination is the most important quality for a true great man. A man who trusts his abilities can't stop anything. This inner confidence is a mental determination that can carry you to the top of any industry.

Next, people have to demonstrate a sense of responsibility. It is an inherent leadership aspect to be able to assume responsibility for anything. Autonomy is a must, too. While externalized needs render you vulnerable to derailment and poverty, if you have your needs from within, then you will always be fulfilled.

Also good guys display good hygiene! Bear in mind, there are no defective mental or religious changes. Watch all the senses, not just looking at them. By general, individuals deemed good by the masses will have social relevance and power; however, these donations are not their own greatness. In fact, your value depends on how well you use your influence. As such, one quantifiable variable is actionable wisdom above all others.

1. He is frank about your problems. Just don't shy and throw them under the rug. If possible, talk about them. Speak when you don't agree with what you say; listen to your voice. Let any woman ask for the balls.

2. He is confident, has faith and is brave. Dismiss with bravery your fears. Make each cell of your body lit with fire and shout to you, "Don't do it!"

3. Balance your life. Balance your life. Make your time a priority. I'm speaking not only with your family and friends in the workplace or the office, but also. If you want to achieve a particular goal, go and determine whether the people in your life play a positive or negative role in achieving that goal. Time is the most important thing in your life that a man can spend.

4. Listen, no matter what you think or think about it. Often by paying attention to someone you can learn a lot. You will still gain a better understanding even if you believe there is nothing to learn. Many people tend to believe that listening simply allows you to be present. It needs energy! It needs commitment!

5. Believe and do anything you dream about. Be an effort, take charge. You will believe it first, if you really want to be the next Michael Jordan. A good man knows the exact kind of person in the future he wants to be. He works continuously for this purpose.

6. Respect yourself and others including animals. A man may yet be male and robust with a feeling of kindness. Including love and cheerfulness, it is good practice to do the right thing. Remember the ancient saying, "What you sow, you catch." There's a fair chance that people would dump you into the garbage if you treat people like trash.

7. Commit to your word. Commit to your word. A good person makes promises, he does not just follow his private protections. A man's good reputation is all. All of this affects: trust in your marriage, financial reputation, and so on. Have a sense of loyalty if you are in a relationship.

8. Know every detail, identify your objectives. A man without objectives is like a seafarer in the seas, without a map. He has no meaning in mind and has no real purpose to waste his time roaming. If you wondered how organized, rich, or successful some people are, here's your response. A person with any ambition must set his goals higher than he feels he can. A fiction may seem like an unrealistic goal, but it will appear increasingly reasonable with time and progress.

9. Know your cash's value. He doesn't let his hard work go into rubbish a good man knows the power of his money. Save for the future and skip the immediate satisfaction of being attached to it is far too simple. Know how to make budget, plan your finances. Recall that a fool will buy all he wants, and a wise man only can buy things he really needs.

10. Have good manners. Have good manners. Your learning is easier, but even more forgetful. Regardless of your personal opinion or view, be considerate to others. A good man neither belittle nor judges his fellow man.

11. Search for information. There's no place to be better than continuous reading. Expand the mind, keep it open for new ideas and concepts. Write, ask and be burning. Read, ask questions.

12. The men he respects are formed by a man. Make this a point of raising and dropping toxic friends occasionally. They deserve no part in your life if they constantly bring you down. Find a mentor, participate in and meet regularly with a close-knit group.

13. Touch yourself and your actions all the time. A good man has a temperance feeling. Before he acts, he thinks without allowing his emotions to take his best. Until pressing, save yourself from future embarrassment, remorse and wrongdoing.

14. Allow privately calm. A good man knows that he does not need public attention to make his point known. Of integrity and reason he resolves disputes. In every situation, he is comfortable and negotiates first with an iron.

15. A guiding vision. The actions of every person influence other people's lives in the future. A good man, whether it's children or adults, is mindful of those around him. In moments of depression and disappointment, it not only inspires them to continue, but helps them. A good man uses his trust to inspire others if they think they have nothing left.

16. I talked and talked I Communication can be a challenge for most men today. In order to clearly express our thoughts and ideas it requires practicality and patience. A decent man can easily express his thoughts and desires.

17. A good introduction. It's no question, it looks important. Regardless of whether we agree with or disagree with it, one thing is certain: a positive image can make wonderful impressions. It means that a good man takes the time to groom and think about what he wears. His introduction corresponds to his personality.

Some More Good Qualities of a Good Man

1. He loves your good qualities and accepts your bad qualities.

You don't feel guilty about faults.

You don't have to hide from him your true self to be what he thinks he wants. You can share your true self, become vulnerable and be sure that it makes him feel closer to you if anything.

2. When you need him, he's there for you, even if it's inconvenient for him.

Often compromises and negotiation are required for a relationship. Life is unforeseen and unpredictable. What will happen you cannot foresee, and anything can go 100% of the time as per expectations. If you need him, he'll be there with you, he will be your partner and will wet the storm with you, though he may want to stay in the sun shines. A husband will be there to you when you need him.

3. Consider you both large and small when making decisions.

A friendship, not a monarchy, is a marriage. Factoring in it shows he respects you, he does not simply envelop you in his world but wants to create a life with you. It isn't always easy to understand someone else's desires and needs as well as expectations, but it is what a partnership is.

4. We all have faults, nobody is flawless. Such faults are not black or white, but the greatest strength of an individual is usually an indication of his greatest weakness. His behavior affects (and vice versa) you in one relationship and sometimes his less developed features affect you negatively. A growing man wants to consolidate and work on his character. A guy that's not oriented towards growth would claim that you have to deal with your problem.

Let's assume that, for example, you are a man who sometimes can be insensitive. Perhaps if you have a tough day he doesn't give you emotional support and only gives you some direct advice. This might be helpful to him at the office if he does not feel like solving problems, but sometimes he does not understand what you are going through and he asks you just what to do about them or is irritated that you're frustrated by something that he doesn't think is so wonderful.

You want a guy who accepts his sound can be harsh, boring and really trying to work on it, not one who says it's your problem and you have to work on it. She won't probably always get it right, but he's going to at least try if he's growing-oriented.

5. General beliefs and principles.

This one is so simple but is ignored so often. You will make sure that both of you are on the same page when it comes to matters of interest when it is your life partner. And if you are not on the same page, make sure he understands where you stand (and vice versa) and that you both work together to achieve an intermediate level that is mutually fulfilling's. This might include religion, core values, preferences about lifestyle, where you want to live, whether you want children.

6. He identifies you as your life partner

This friendship is more than just you and him... you and he are a team together. And as this squad, you are both stronger individually than you can be. He sees you as his equal. Not a person there to feed his ego, validate him, be his emotional crutch and be here to suit his needs. He considers himself to be a valuable man.

He values all about you—your feelings, goals, beliefs, what you say, your business, your work. It doesn't make you feel bad about your life and he appreciates the person you are and your choices.

7. He is ready to make efforts in this regard.

He wants to work hardened, to be stronger, to be his best self if there's a problem, to find a way to resolve it. What is important to remember is that people have different ideas of what effort means in a relationship. He may feel that hard work and good at his job is hard to make because he wants to provide you with nice things and a comfortable lifestyle (I am taking this as an example because this is a common point of contention between men and women because she often finds him working too hard to be married to his job).

8. You can communicate among yourselves.

Even about tough problems and even if someone gets upset.

With the right man, for fear of rocking your boat, you won't be afraid of sailing certain things. You know that he respects you, and you see as valid and important what you have to say. All relationships face their number of barriers. There will be battles, misunderstandings, arguments and times when a partner does not feel like that. The only way to emerge better and stronger from difficult times is to deal with them, and this starts with open communication.

He is trustworthy. He's safe.

You feel secure and honest with him and you do not fear that he violates or uses anything against you. You are confident that he will not leave you unexpectedly, that he is genuine, that what he says does mean. You have no sense of suspicion underlying it, as if it had any further motive. You are assured that he cares deeply about you and never harms you deliberately.

10. He wants to marry you. He wants to spend the rest of his life with you.

So, that appears so clear, but it's still not. A guy could have all the qualities, but if he wouldn't marry you or if he mightn't want to marry, he wouldn't be your husband. He knows early on when a man is ready to marry and meet a girl with whom he feels he will spend his life. That's not to say they're engaged immediately, but he knows that, and perhaps he says that it's so obvious to her or he doesn't even have to. He knows this and she knows it. It might be an incorrect moment, maybe he wants to wait before he gets more financially stable and established in his profession, but he still transmits his level of commitment, he won't hang up, guess, and wonder.

If he still feels as though he's got wild oats to sow and still is attracted to the lifestyle, bachelor and party boy, he's no friend, and you'll be disappointed. If you are serious and lasting about what you want, make sure you are on the same page before you do anything. It is usually quite apparent when a man is ready for a serious undertaking. And then take it up and talk to him if it's not. He will understand if he's a husband's stuff. If he's not... you know at least now that it is too late before.

Some Attributes of a Good Man as an Ideal Husband

1. The love He gives you as his wife is the love you deserve. He loves you, he respects you. He hugs and embraces you. No matter how many years have passed, he is caring and loving to you.

2. Independence: He does not depend on his parents or parents to provide food, shelter and other family needs for you and your children. He's working hard to give you your own home.

3. Leadership: He is trustworthy, takes initiative and knows how to guide your family along the right road. You know you can't be lost in life when you are with him. For this reason you are prepared to be his girlfriend. You are willing. For your children, it's also a good role model.

4. He doesn't cheat on you and is very loyal to you. He doesn't flirt with other girls. He is worried that he will lose you if he will do any such thing

5. You must not worry about him, Self-Love, because you know he can take care of himself. It's just as he loves you and your parents, he loves himself. He tries to be happy and healthy so that for you and your children he can always be there.

6. Confidence: He has faith in you. He doesn't treat you like a tricker, he trusts you. He also gives you all of his possessions, cash, and recurring pay.

7. Knowledge He trusts you because he knows you better than anybody else in connection with He has tried to know you. He knows your favorite color, music, food, location—and he knows everything about you as well. He's interested in always knowing you.

8. Honesty, transparency and Truthfulness: He has faith in you, and in return, you should trust him too.

9. He doesn't forget to thank you, thanks. Just small things you do for him he appreciates. And because of that, because you know your efforts will not be wasted you are more inspired to serve and to love him.

10. He treats you and his children with patience and doesn't get angry easily. If problems or issues occur, he doesn't get easily upset. He is able to tolerate pain or suffering as he knows that they are all just trials that should make him stronger than weaker.

11. It is persistent and uniform. He'll never stop for you and your family until he's realizing his dream. He isn't discouraged, and even his several attempts fail, he doesn't give up. He will continue to provide your family with a better future regardless of how complicated or how long it will take

12. He has Self-control and is autonomous. He knows how to control himself to protect his life from smoke, drunkenness, idleness, lust and any other vices.

13. He can discern from the wrong what is right. He's not a stupid ignorant man who keeps committing wrongdoing, like lying, cheating, being irresponsible, lazy and thinking they're okay.

14. You he understands comprehension. He knows himself. He understands himself. He knows what he's talking about. His options or actions he knows. He knows because he does what he preaches and experiences.

15. Compassion: As he is compassionate so he understands you. And he wants you to stay happy, he feels your joy. And he feels your sorrow and sorrow, so he wants to do all he can to alleviate your pain.

16. He's not avenging for salvation. He's not catching the errors and looking back. You and your children know how to forgive, forget and live a joyous life.

17. Just: He refuses evil. He leaves sins, evil, and corruption. He's doing what's right, and he's grateful for that. His legitimate deeds bring you and the lives of your children good karma.

18. Righteousness: He is just and honest. He never makes you feel that it's so unfair to live with him.

19. Respectful: As a woman, he respects you. While different from his, he values your own views and choices. He can respect himself as well.

20. Happiness and Satisfaction: He is happy and satisfied with you. You are true to him, his dream. He never wants other women or girlfriends. He doesn't want other people because he knows for him he's the lucky man on Earth, because he's the one who has you.

21. He has a sense of commitment and selflessness. He puts you first and before himself, he thinks about you and your kids. For you, he gives up his own stuff. For the entire family, not just himself, it spends his money, time and energy. You will find no reason to call him an egotist.

22. He is a person afraid of God. Godhead. His teachings of creation are obeyed by God's orders and followed. You and your children are brought closer to God.

23. He always sees with you a good future, no matter how hard it is. Despite your shortcomings and limitations, he doesn't easily lose faith. It provides you with good vibes that make your home and family happier, more confident and always go no matter how difficult life is.

24. He's true to you, fidelity. He believes in you. He believes in you. He doesn't have to see you to believe you all the time. He doesn't have to know everything about you to believe you. His faith is at play—he listens to you, loves you and sacrifices for you because of his reality.

25. Diligent: For you he's working hard. He is driven to work for your children to build a brighter future. They don't waste time, but they are doing their work or livelihood continuously and passionately so that your family can always reap in the future.

26. Benevolent: He's a boy with a goodness of soul. He wants to help you always and he wants to see you smile. He's not mean. He's not rude. He won't harm you physically, mentally and emotionally.

27. Gentle: He treats your spirit, your soul, and your body sweetly and gently. He reproves you gently and calmly, not furiously if you make mistakes.

28. He does not like quarrels and narrow struggles. If you're not in a good mode, he doesn't argue with you. Whenever you need it, it gives you time and space. He must find the right time to speak and to hear you solve the problems so that you both can sleep well.

29. He's not arrogant and proud. Humility He is a strong person of mind, heart and emotion — and that's why he can manage to transcend pride and encourage the people around him to show kindness, peace and happiness.

30. Accepting you for who you are: He accepts you and doesn't judge you. He doesn't judge you. He's not obliging you to be a guy you're not. But as a better person, he continues to inspire you. He encourages you to make the better change by showing you the change that he wants you to be.

31. It helps you in your efforts to become a better and better woman. He also helps your children make their own life decisions as long as he sees them as just and happy.

32. True love: He's really in love with you, finally. He knows it, he is sure, he feels it, and he tells you always, even in odd times and places, about his true feelings.

It is difficult to find the qualities of a good husband that I mentioned earlier. But if a man really loves a woman or his wife, he must try to build up the above qualities. Therefore, is true love not unifying all of them, is it?

Chapter 3

Ways to figure out that you are in Love

It feels different for everyone to know you're in love. Some have often been in love and know well the feeling, and some may not be sure whether it's love or a deep enthusiasm.

Luckily, your body has some pretty sneaky ways to tell you that this is more than a passing phase for your mate. Keep an eye on the signs of these myths the next time you doubt whether you're in love. You can't stop looking at it. It can be a sign that you're head over heels if your partner has ever caught you looking at them lovingly. Eye contact means you're connected to something, and you may just be in love if you notice your eyes fixed to your friend.

Research have showed that couples that lock their eyes feel more romantically related than those that don't. It also goes the other way: when a study had strangers clinging their eyes for minutes, they reported a romantic feeling. It's completely normal to feel out of your mind when you fall for someone. You know that you're high. A study by the Kinsey Institute found that a love-dweller's brain is the same as that of a cocaine-dweller. You should thank dopamine for this sensation, which is released in both situations. This is a good reason why people can be totally absurd in new relationships.

When you love somebody, you can feel like you can't get them off your mind. You think about them. That's because when you fall into love with someone, your brain releases phenylthylamine, sometimes called a "heart medicament." This hormone gives your partner a sense of enthusiasm.

You may know the feeling, because phenylethylamine is found in chocolate, which can explain why after one square you cannot stop. You want them to be happy. Love is an equal partnership, but you will find that when you fall for them, happiness is really important to you.

According to study, so-called "compassionate charity" can be one of the strongest indicators of good relations. This means you're prepared to leave your way to make life easier and happier for your partner. If your partner walks in the rain or makes them breakfast in a busy morning on a weekday, it's a sign that you have it bad.

Lately, you were stressed. Love can be a source of stress, though often associated with warm and fluffy feelings. Being amateur also causes the stress hormone cortisol to escape from your brain and can make you feel the sun. If you realize that you have tested your patience or you freak out, you probably won't have to wear a stress ball yet; you may just be in love. If that is a little bit more than normal.

You do not feel so painful. Falling for someone could be painful, but it might be a big sign you're in love if you've noticed that literally falling won't disturb you.

A study carried out by Stanford University School of Medicine has shown that participants are looking at a picture of someone they love, that mild pain can be reduced by up to 40% and extreme pain can be reduced by up to 15%.

So you may want to keep an image of your partner handy if you get a tattoo. Only if so. You try new stuff.

At the beginning of their relationships, everybody wants to impression their date, but if you continually try new things your partner likes, you may have been bitten by the love bug.

In fact, a study found that after these relationships people who claimed to be in love had often different interests and personalities. So even if you dislike your partner for the square-dancing class, this could have a positive impact on your personality.

Their heart rate syncs with your heart rate.

When you think of the one you love, your heart might skip a beat, but a study showed you can beaten with each other in time. A study by the University of California, Davis, shows that when people love, couples ' hearts start to beat at the same rate.

You are fine with Gross Stuff as well

While you may not know if it was without a few stethoscopes, it's a good sign that you have a deep connection with your partner. With the big stuff, you're OK. If after just watching you pick the nose, you are famous for the germaphobe and totally cool to kiss your partner, you might just be in love. Indeed, a study from the University of Groningen in the Netherlands found that sexual excitement can override feelings.

This means you can only encourage them to double down if you are super attracted to your partner. This is love, darling. That's love. If you're nauseous and sweaty, you either have a bad belly bug or fall in love. You're sweater. One study showed that falling in love can lead to sickness and to physical symptoms, such as sweat, similar to anxiety or stress. While it'll probably happen when your partner is really relaxed, it's a good idea to have an extra hanky, just to be healthy.

If you really meet someone, you may choose the small stuff that makes them unique. You love their quirks. And if you're in love with them, this is probably some of the things you're most interested in.

A study found that small quirks actually can make a person love more deeply than physically because people have unique preferences. So, although your partner may have judged you harshly at first glance, you might be in love if you find that you are suddenly astonished at their uniqueness.

Yes, you are falling in Love!!!

Can't you get out of your mind the girl or the guy? When should you be working, Day dreaming about the person? Envisioning together your future? These vertiginous thoughts can be signs of love.

Indeed, scientists have defined exactly what "fallen in love" means. Researchers have found that an amorous brain is very different from a person who has simple desires and is also different from a brain of someone who's in a long-term, committed relationship. Study by Helen Fisher, a Rutgers University anthropologist and one of the leading biological love experts, revealed that the "in love" stage of the brain is an unparalleled and well-defined time-span. You start to think your beloved is special when you're in love.

The belief is combined with a belief that nobody else can feel a romantic passion. Fisher and her colleagues believe that this is the result of high levels of central dopamine— a chemical that is deeply affected and concentrated — in your brain. People in love tend to concentrate on their beloved's positive qualities while ignoring his or her negative characteristics. We also focus on banal activities and items that remind them of their loved one who dreams of these precious moments and memories. Such intense attention is also expected to result from the elevated central dopamine levels and the spike of norepinephrine, which is a chemical in the presence of new stimuli, associated with increased memory.

As is well known, falling into love also leads to physiological and emotional instability. You bounce between anticipation, euphoria, increased energy, lack of sleep, loss of appetite, sweating, a pounding heart and a quick breath, as well as fear, nausea, and feelings of depression in the slightest setback. This mood is similar to drug addicts ' behavior. Yes, when loving people have pictures of their loved ones, the same brain regions fire up when a pharmacist arrives. Love is a form of addiction, researchers say. Any other person experiencing some type of adversity tends to enhance romantic attraction. Central dopamine may also be responsible for this reaction, because research shows that, if a reward is delayed, neurons generating dopamine become more active in the mid-brain region.

Those in love report spending on their "love object," according to Fisher, an average of 85% of their waking hours considering it. Intrusive thought, as this form of obsessive behavior, may result from lower levels of central serotonin in the brain, which was previously associated with obsessive behavior. People in love regularly show signs of emotional dependence on their connection, including possessiveness, jealousy, fear of refusal, and anxiety about separation. (Obsessive-compulsive disorder is treated with serotonine recovery inhibitors). For example, Fisher and her colleagues looked at individuals ' brains looking at pictures of a loved one that was rejected or someone they were still in love with after that person had rejected it. Functional MRI activity was shown in many areas of the brain, including forebrain areas, shown to play a role in cocaine cravings. In 2010 the researchers wrote in the Neurophysiology Journal that' the activation of cocaine addictions areas may help to explain obsessive behavior associated with love rejection.' I also want a close and daydreaming friendship with their loved ones and try ways to get closer.

Another specialist in passion, Lucy Brown, neuroscientist at the New York Albert Einstein College of Medicine, says it's like a pull towards water and other stuff that we need to live.

Functional IRD research shows that simple neural primitive structures, such as the one that gives us hunger or thirst, are involved in almost everybody when looking at their beloved face and thinking about loving thoughts. "Brown told Live Science in 2011."I believe that romantic love is a component of human reproductive strategy, and that it helps us to build relationships which help us to survive.

Persons who are lovers usually feel deep compassion for their loved ones, feel the pain of the other person as their own and are prepared, for the other person, to sacrifice something. Fallen in love is characterized by a desire to reorganize your everyday goals and/or change your clothes, mannerisms, behaviors or beliefs in order to suit your beloved better.

But being a person can also be your greatest bet: she found that people attracted to their opposite, at least the' brain-chemical' opposites, in yet another study by Fishers, presented in 2013 at the' Being Human ' conference. For example, their research has found that people with the so-called testosterone-dominant personalities (very logical, competitive and emotional) have often attracted mates with high estrogen and oxytocin-linked personalities–they appear to be "empathic, caring, trustworthy, pro-social" and introspective people who seek meaning and identity, It is believed that this possessiveness has evolved so that the lover will make his or her partner spur other followers and thus make sure the court order is not interrupted until conception takes place. Although the desire for sexual union is important for lovers, the desire for emotional union prevails. The report says that "Sex is the most important part of my relationship with my partner." Fisher and her colleagues found that people who claim to be "in the love" commonly say that their passion is unintentional and unacceptable.

The late psychologist Dorothy Tennov asked 400 Connecticuters to respond to her book "Love and Limerence" in 1979, which included 200 comments on love. Many of the participants said their fascination was irrational and unconscious, voicing feelings of helplessness. Accommodation is not safe. According to Fisher, a researcher, business manager, wrote about a bureau crush in the early 50's.' I am advancing into this study that this desire for Emily is a sort of natural, instinct-like behavior that is not under voluntary or rational command.

Chapter 4

Love changes a person in many ways

Psychological Changes

Have you ever looked lovingly at your partner and felt your heart sweat, palms sweat, or mood getting better immediately? This is because falling into love really changes your body's events— for the better. Neurochemicals such as dopamine and oxytocin flood our brains in love in areas associated with pleasure and reward, producing physical and psychological responses such as lower perception of pain, addiction and an increase in sexual desire.

Cuddling, hugging, and kissing your loved one can quickly reduce stress and boost feelings of calmer, comfortable and healthy thanks to oxytocin. Your mood will improve due to the influx of dopamine at the reward center.

Here are seven ways when you fall in love, your body and brain change. Higher blood pressure or high blood pressure is a dangerous condition which makes your body more vulnerable to heart attack, stroke and kidney failure. Medications and changes in lifestyle such as exercise and healthier eating can control or reduce hypertension, but research has also suggested a natural way of reducing your blood pressure.

In the US Department of Health Services ' study published in 2007, married couples had reduced blood pressure and lower risk of cardiovascular disease and looked at the relationship of marriage to physical health and longevity.

The American College of Cardiology examined 3.5 million individual, divorced or widowed persons in an analysis of risk of cardiovascular diseases. We found that the risk for married couples under 50 years of age was typically 12% lower. Couples aged 51 to 60 years had a 7% lower risk of illness compared to their unmarried counterparts. Falling for someone may at the outset be stressful— whether they feel the same way, the chance of rejection, and the fear when those three big words are to be said, is not uncertain.

According to a small study published in 2004, the initial stages of love decrease increase the levels of cortisol, a stress hormone, in new couples. The cortisol levels were, however, returned to normal after participants had been checked from 12 to 24 months later.

While love for some — especially in the first stages — can be stressful, it can in the long run reduce stress. The neurobiology of those in love was investigated by Neuroendocrinology Letters, a study published in 2005, which found a link between the stress response mechanisms of people called activation of HPA axis and development of social attachment. The results suggest that establishing a connection with your partner can lead to physiological changes which reduce anxiety levels.

One reason you feel less depressed is that you feel safe in love and build trust in your loved one.

According to a Harvard Medical School report, oxytocin, an hormone released via physical contact such as hugging, kissing, and sex, enhances feelings of attachment to your partners and generates feelings of happiness, calmness and security.

In social bonds, maternal instinct and reproduction as well as sexual pleasure oxytocin also plays a major role. According to a research published in Nature, the "love hormone" significantly increases social connection and trust among partners. Have you ever felt the acceleration of your heartbeat, palms or stomach churn (well done) when you were looking or think about someone you love? In love, the level of cortisol rises and the body flies or flies.

Dr. Daniel Amen, a mental health psychiatrist and neuroscientist, told NBC News "Your limbic or emotional brain activates a vagus nerve going from your brain to your gut. "When you become nervous or are excited, this nerve is stimulated, which activates the gut," he says. He releases dopamine, a new neurotransmitter that controls the rewards of your brains and the fun center, making a pair feel happy with themselves. "If I tell my patients that is the same sensation." It does depend on your interpretation.

In a 2005 study in The Journal of Comparative Neurology, 2 500 brain images of seventeen people who describing themselves as in love were analyzed. Researchers found that participants who looked at a romantically appreciated photo of an individual showed a caudate and a ventralized segmentation in two areas highly linked to dopamine. LOVE can be addictive in itself like addiction drugs that illuminate our centers of pleasure and keep people returning for more.

Wissenschaftlers have found similar neurochemical reactions in people with drug dependence and love within the same areas of the brain. The research on the relation between addiction and love was reviewed in a study published in 2017 in Philosophy, Psychiatry, and Psychography.

The authors suggested that love can be addictive, because a need can be temporarily met, but it can be very distracting when it is not met for a long time. However, some of these feelings may be related to sex — sexual activity, orgasms, and some medications release dopamine in an area of the brain called the nucleus accumbens (official Medical Classification Guides do not include love as addiction). Oxytocin and serotonin rush and muscle relaxation of an orgasm will leave you looking for more. That's why it could feel like you can rush into sexual activity.

How your First Love Changes your Personality

1. Through someone else's eyes you continue to see yourself and often wonder what you could do to be a better person for them.

2. Even if you know they should not, the schedule and needs of somebody else are more important than your own.

3. You know what in a relationship you can and can't tolerate. (You know, too, that if you really love the person— but that's a bad idea to do so] you will tend to bend these things.) For the first time, someone becomes more attractive to you than your body, and you know that what they look like is their least important thing.

5. It all begins to seem secondary, including stuff that you were fully interested in, to experience love with someone.

6. You get in raw, unfiltered moments that can only be taken out by someone who loves you.

7. You know that having a crush and love is special, because you can raise or disregard all the non-practical or unnecessary aspects of what it would mean to be with them in a crush.

8. Without actually realizing that you accept (or imitate) new recipes, cultures, music and jokes, you absorb them in your personality entirely new. You have always said that you won't be that guy, but you are absolutely obsessed with what your SO likes.

9. What you do really with this person is far less important than that you are with them in your life for the first time.

10. After you first meet the parents, you begin to realize that it is not at once as frightening as you felt it was and infinitely scarier than you might have expected.

11. You learn what healthy struggle means, and you fight for something longer than just who wins this argument.

12. You are part of a team and can understand that you disagree with something, although you both want what the other one wants at the end of the day.

13. Then. The night has not slept because you haven't heard from your SO, it's becoming more a reality and a ridiculous image of the desperate person.

14. They understand that it might not be enough to love and want to be with someone above all to transcend fundamental differences.

15. Your friends are starting to see you as a couple rather than a single person and they are saying how fun it is to see you and yourself during the nights when you end up going out.

16. The person you love is going to break your heart and even though that is always the end of the world, you realize that life is not finished.

17. You also find that the more potent relations often take several false beginnings before you can finally break up.

18. Though you love this person so much, in the end, you love yourself more and want to protect what you have had before you fell into love first of all.

19. Because of everything that you told your first love, you are willing to find someone new to share everything with, even when you are head-over-heels again, you won't be that disappointed.

How Love Changes our Personalities for Better?

You not only feel good inside, but you feel different outside being in love.

The song "You Look So Good in Love" was famous for Country Music superstar George Strait. As we heard his beautiful masterful song, we wondered: Do the loving people look the same as the loving people who do not look?

We have concluded that the answer is a rounding no (based on our 32 years ' experience in love and marriage expertise). We start to change for the better when people fall in love. Though at times love is difficult, it's good for you to be in love with someone.

So, when in love, what do you look like? Our investigation suggests:

1. You are happy. You are happier.

You smile and laugh more when you're in love. With your love and the world you feel happy. You feel happy. From ear to ear all makes you grin.

It turns out, happy people in the relationship say that "happiness" is the precursor to love. So now begin to practice your happy face!

See how long do you take to fall in love for your tango for your relationship advice?

2. You are more trustworthy.

If you're in love, you're standing a bit bigger and feel confident. Don't make mistakes— you feel good about yourself in life. In your own skin, you feel good.

And even if you face rejection, you are happy to accept that choice.

3. You look better. You look good looking.

You can notice on the outside the lit feeling you get indoors. When you are in love, you are noticeably nicer or more beautiful.

Sometimes when you try to look best for the one you love— you choose more flattering clothes, style your hair nicer, etc. But it also helps make your hair brighter and give your skin a sweet light by releasing love chemicals in your flesh.

4. You are taking additional risks.

While love is full of risks, lovers are healthier and easier. In fact, your worry seems to disappear. You are ready to take opportunities and confidence in another human. Finally, you will pay dividends for giving you joy by investing in someone you trust.

5. You are more affectionate. More passionate.

Okay, you're not suddenly the snuggest person? Sure, that's what love is going to do for you. If you are in love, you are more easily caring for others (and not just your interests in love), you are more often hugging and more authentic.

To truly and completely love another makes you a more caring person. No doubt about it: people who are in love are more affectionate and loving. Everyone around you (including this colleague you just hugged) notices.

For many wonderful reasons, people in love "look so good in bed." So smile, stand tall, and snuggle away— you're sure of that easy-going joy.

Chapter 5:

Lifetime Commitment in a Love Relationship

The greatest challenge for a couple is to find a rhythm in a relationship. When you meet someone (prior to the relationship, it's really hard to find a person!), you are easy to fall in love. "I love you," is easy to say, once a boyfriend or girlfriend has a special moment.

But what about that coherence that we all want from true engagement? What about it? It's a lot more difficult. It is possible, however. Commitment starts with wishful thinking. Each person must want it and be prepared to make sacrifices for the other person. The way we look at ourselves and give up something to give to someone else is changing. It's not as hard a matter, as you could imagine.

We're a little less dedicated than our parents and older generations of centuries. Purchase a house, settle down and find someone special. We wouldn't be hurried to remember. To support this, there is a startling study from the Pew Research Center: "The Pew Research Center estimates that thousands are much less likely to be married in their 20s than previous generations.

The figure from 18 to 29 years old who said they were single and did not live with a partner was increased by 52%, in 2004, to 64%, and in 2014, according to a recent survey by Gallup. In the same decade, the marriage between 30 people decreased by 10 percentage points while the rate of living together increased from 7 to 13 percent. I'm an example of this research living, breathing.

A lack of commitment to a partner characterized many of my 20s. The relationship I had to get right through all of the time, the relationship with me was the relationship I had to get right. You need to be right before you can truly expect to commit to another human.

My mother and I are opposed to each other in most ways. My emotions and feelings are much more open to me. She tends to maintain them. Both of us show different aspects of our emotional intelligence. It takes me socially to get relaxed in a crowd a little longer, but then I'm completely extrovert. The social butterfly at galas and large social meetings is my wife's most introverted.

That's what we challenge!

I think it depends really on the version of the story you want to trust when I have time to engage on my wife. The night she met me, my wife knew that "I was the one." No joke.-No joke. I had to work it out much longer. In partnership, I haven't been thinking. I have not been up. I have not been ready.

What I have learned from this experience is that commitment requires both an "all-in" mentality and open communication channels. Relationships require each person to live up to the current and the future with a twofold commitment. Nothing is surely promised, but it's crucial for communication to take place when it comes to progressing in a relationship and talking marriage.

Marriage is the life-long covenant.

And, what about you, what about you? How are you going to know when to commit? How do you know what this will mean by reaching a compromise between loving and continuing with all your heart and repeatedly?

It was through my experience, study of other and scientific studies that I established the five key elements for the commitment. I hope it's good for you. Please let the comments know your thoughts!

1. Great trust and commitment builders are a shared and positive experience in a relationship with the person you are loving. Think about how you and your partner see your relationship as it is. I bet you share in your inner joke with your partner came from that day on the baseball game, or from the moment your boyfriend forgot his wallet. I bet you shared with your partner. Oops! Oops! Oops! Now for this mishap he's eternally grilled!

Yet we remember these things! Take the funny and negative things and make them good experiences. And you can experience positive experiences, experience the memories and build new experiences.

My wife and I still joke together at graduate school about our first date. She is the more fitting south kid. I was the rough-round-northerner bottom. She couldn't literally believe I decided to go for a nice pizzeria in "Dutch." We have divided the bill. I was going to pick up the tab, she thought. Yeah, we're still joking. And I'm not apologetic yet!

Did you worry about spending $1000 on this journey to Florida? Go for that. Go for that. It'll always last, and describe your relationships, from the happy interactions-memories. You are building engagement.

2. The main objective of this approach is "all in" in thought, words and actions. I heard the speaker say, "You're here, during a speech recently. You're here. You're here. Be there, therefore. Work hard!-Work hard! "That's right. Take work for relationships! It will be fast, smooth days, but conflict and fighting will also occur!

It's your time with your partner that I'm getting to. Worth that moment. Worth this moment. We share so precious moments with the people we love. Think of what makes that person happy. Go "all in." Consider ways to improve your relationship, fun stuff or tasks to reduce your burden.

Speak, show your affection and claim that you care for your boyfriend or girlfriend. Above all, show that you are careful. Actions are always more loud than words, but it doesn't mean words and thoughts are important. That's what helps your actions. So go ahead—get your basketball boyfriend's tickets. Get flowers for your girlfriend. Tell your loving partner. Let them know that in your life they are the most important person.

Eliminating distractions and trials: The guy who has checked out your number at the bar and asked for a good hour's job? Think it. Forget about it. Stay late in the evening to watch your friend's YouTube video? A slow assassin. These are things that break apart relationships, trials and minor distractions. And it isn't the big-bang approach exactly most of the time. The road to ruin is slower, slower and pernicious.

Dr John Lydon of McGill University talked about a study showing pictures of opposite sex women and men. The person they found attractive was told to remember. It really got interesting then. "The more engaged you were," says Dr. Lydon, "the less appealing it was that you found some other people threatened your connection." To be loyal and committed to my girlfriend, I had to remove the tentations, like those of the New York Times, I said more: "When they were drawn to someone who might challenge your marriage, they immediately thought," It's not too nice. All of us are vulnerable to allow our eyes and minds to wander. Factors like alcohol, emotionally charged incentives and tiredness can all help to make us vulnerable.

Take the picture of these things. It calls for discipline, but then a friendship again.

We'll always see it first through our own eyes, willingness to understand things from the point of view of your friend. This is life fact. However, it's an intention to understand the needs, desires and views of your partner that separated great relationships from mediocre ones. You must throw out your ego and understand where it comes from.

There is nothing more you need than one person when you emotionally struggle with fear, concern or a sense of inadequacy. Your partner's commitment meets your requirements. Be a great listener. Be a great listener. Do something kind. Make something kind. You are always keen to understand your point of view!

What is the most important thing that I'll be the first to tell you, spontaneity is part of what makes things beautiful and the accidental, momentary things that make the relationship special should always be celebrated. However, it is even more important to talk to yourself and as a couple-for the sake of longevity. These two things are different!

I love to write, teach and watch baseball Yankees. My wife loves clothing for girls and home decor. We understand the meaning of our personal time for us. Together with our son and we also love doing things that please us.

At the end of the day, focus on the things you really need. Make sure your enthusiasm and passions come out! This is so important to reach the commitment agreement.

Love and Commitment form the basis of a lifetime relationship

Find your ego's and your essence's responsibilities. The ego wants to commit itself to nothing—a position, a relationship, a job—because it believes something better will happen. And it is ready to forget what is present because something better is not present. It's not present. Essence is committed to anything, on the other hand. It does not invest in the future because the present is all that remains.

The ego dreams about anything better amidst anything, and the essence simply likes and commits attention and love to anything. This is the main difference between ego and essence. Ultimately, dwelling on anything present contributes to pleasure.

This is why the ego enjoys so little-it pays attention to and suffers not to pay attention to what is not present and what is not. She loves her visions, her dreams and desires more than she wants.

To love, we must love reality—what is true right now, and not what could be true in the future or what we want to be true in the future. In the present, love happens (like all, really). Therefore, the ego does not know about love—because love is the experience of now or now. When the ego experiences it now, it's running out of it.

Commitment requires a desire to fall in love with life— with your real partner — rather than searching for anything else, either in reality or through imagination. What you are committed to right now is what is here. Who knows next what's going to be here? All you've ever got is what's right now here, so it makes sense to participate in this, to give your full attention to this—your affection.

Those who have trouble engaging in a relationship often have difficulty committing themselves to other things. I have a conviction that what's not good enough here and that what's better somewhere else. This is the fundamental assumption of the ego about life: It is not what happens now. It's there, with ultimate happiness and pleasure.

The ego assumes that it is not good enough because it sees everything that happens. It then suggests that something else is going to be good enough. Ego conceives of peace and happiness one day because life is finally well aligned. Those who cannot commit always wait for life to come into being, and they are sure that the vision of the future does not look like any life now.

The funny thing (or nothing so funny) is that life rarely suits someone simply because the ego will not see it as' lines up.' Even if it's quite good, life has the habit of perceiving it to be imperfect. Life is not meant in any case to be perfect or to fulfill the desires and dreams of the ego. It has a higher purpose, which has nothing too much to do with the desires of the ego. Life is basically about learning how to live and learn a lot more. And this is why life is less than ideal for the ego.

For different reasons, life brings people into our lives. We must sometimes be ready to stretch out to gain what is made of a relationship or to use the love that is possible. Like life, relationship, although they can be profoundly rewarding, is not meant to be easy.

Commitment allows the ability of a partnership to be fulfilled. You may never know this opportunity when you give up on a relationship after the first flush is gone. Sexual union often turns into the glue that keeps people together long enough to experience true love or learn from one another. Nature has a way of learning religious and social growth. Sexual attraction is one way that Essence unites people and holds them together for as long as possible to benefit and grow from each other.

The ego doesn't value development, and for that or for love it's not in relation. His unwillingness to commit themselves and to grow often prevents that relationship from becoming very well. The perfect "10," which doesn't exist, is chasing forever. However, it's hard to persuade the ego. It believes in its imaginations. It is just a matter of time for the ego before "this" happens. Eternal hope comes forth.

Essence encounters "the one" that appears, and that's how Essence varies from the ego. You will love anyone who appears in your life. Yes, if you want to be satisfied, it's very wise to do so. You only reject those who appear in your life if you don't want to be happy.

You shouldn't be racist, it doesn't say. To love and to say yes to those who come up in your life doesn't mean to engage with them if you don't. Essence tells them yes—its accessible—it's interesting. And then it's very smart to get more involved. Essence is committed to someone only if love flows both ways and the relationship on many levels is rewarding. The ego, on the other hand, can become sexually attractive or because this relationship does not serve as a good basis for commitment to meet some other necessity.

Commitment is only valid if love exists. Nonetheless, the ego can't love. It forms needs-based relationships that fail to be committed. Once the needs of someone are not met, the dedication is called into question. Those associated with the ego most times have a very difficult time, whilst those identified with Essence will love and therefore commit.

Commitment flows of course through love and another's appreciation. This is the natural result of passion. And this love is often sufficient to overcome conditioning and other difficulties in the relationship. Engagement is hollow without love; there is no base. Without passion, weather conditions and other challenges will not be strong enough to establish the relationship.

Ultimately all people learn to love, but when egos are in control, relationships can be quite unpredictable. Yet because the relationships give the ego many of the practical aspects that it needs—gender, health, intimacy, empathy, support and assistance—people who, for egoisms, also discover love in relationships. So life draws people from the ego and into the essentials.

Chapter 6:

Ways to figure out that he is really committed to you.

Commitment in a Relationship

I hear from so many of you the same thing, and it's the same thing I used to say not so long ago.

I hear you say you want a guy to pledge yourself. You would like to have a guy who's committed to you. You wonder if a man who really needs to have a devotion will ever find you.

You might want to know if he wants a committed relationship or if he'll be a stringer (that is, a fellow who only holds you together for years to finally break it down), or perhaps you've been stuck for a long time and you want to know how to get him to actually make a commitment.

Or you might be single, and you want to know how to find a man who is ready to engage, because all the people you have met have proven to be phenomena of commitment.

This is one of the biggest questions on our minds for all these reasons and much more.

My question to you is this: What do you think of a committed relationship?

What is the real meaning of engagement? Have you ever sat down and really considered exactly what you want a committed relationship to be, when you say? If you think you want to commit a guy?

It didn't most of us.

It is really so difficult to describe the prevalence of a living together before marriage, especially in our modern cultural textualization, hanging out and hanging up.

In the past, things were slightly sliced and dry (i.e. on your grandmother's day). Engagement meant that you were married with a ring on the left and a wedding date. Unless they were officially engaged, most women would not even find a partner exclusive. They were "court" until then, and she (as well as he) could date / court as many as she chose.

It's a lot different today. They now have phrases such as "friends with benefits" to let us know how times vary. Here are a couple of examples of committed relationships that I have learned when I inquire what that means: you and your partner are exclusive, meaning that neither of you dates. The word will apply regardless of whether you are intimate or not.

While that is certainly a major part of a committed relation (and is indeed the start of a committed long-term relationship), I would prefer to call it simply' exclusive' rather than' engaged.' Commitment means far more than exclusivity. Exclusive means only that neither of you will date other people, but it can end so quickly, particularly if any of you have not updated your Tinder or Match.com profile.

To be the first step in a committed relationship, you and your partner must be closed to other possibilities–both online and physically.

But what about "hanging out" (especially one that is very attractive), or an ex-friend of the opposite sex?

This is where you are still 100% committed to making the relationship work. This means that no matter what happens, you put energy into doing it, and you are both driven to be together over the long distance.

This is usually the second stage of a committed marriage, in which some magic is starting to vanish and you both note each other's shortcomings (and all of a sudden his flaws have become so molest). It is here that you begin to understand that you do not actually agree with certain issues.

In this way many of these so-called committed relations (which were really a temporary exclusiveness agreement) collapse and collapse. This is where some compromise begins to be needed. This is also where genuine engagement begins because it means that you both are willing to work out things instead of breaking up with the first sign of anything that does not look like the fairy tale.

Deepening this engagement is again too long as it follows the stage of "dedication." It probably doesn't mean anything when you've engaged you in the Bahamas after a 2 week whirlwind romance.

Of course, commitments can still be broken, so this is not a guaranteed long-term commitment, but it's still the best sign for you that things go that way.

Also, it is based on your engagement–some people get engaged but never set a date or plan a wedding–before you realize that you've been involved for three years and that you're no closer to saying, "I do." I believe that his activities are important at this stage: the more he participates actively in the planning of the marriage, the more dedicated he is to the relationship.

Marriage most people feel that this marriage isn't really committed until you both exchange your vows and say, "I do." Marriage although divorce in most cultures is a choice, it does not become a further deepening of the relationship physically, emotionally or financially.

On the other hand, you may feel that you do not have to be married to feel committed. Those partners had long-standing and unmarried relationships (think Goldie Hawn and Kurt Russel or Oprah Winfrey and Steadman Graham).

Is that even a guarantee of complete commitment when you are married? I don't think so–marrying and having a ring on the left is just a symbol of engagement–true engagement in your life together, every day, where nearly anything you do has a bearing upon each other.

Living and devoted this is not just where you are living, but 100 percent (i.e. divorce is out of the question). This strengthens the commitment to the relationship, which I hope was present in the previous stage.

But there are different, deeper, more subtle definitions within each of these definitions. It's really a tricky thing to do here.

Like: to be part of the lives of each other. When he spends his holidays with his family, for example, is it okay if he shows up and spends the day watching the football game on the couch? Or would you like him to spend that time meeting your family and getting involved in all their life-related issues or discussions?

What is the point of independence? Do you like to be a "girls ' weekend," or at least a girl's night out now and then? You like a woman who loves her own freedom. Do you like meeting with your own mates to lunch or coffee once a week? What about opposite sex friends? Would you okay go hanging out with a friend (or working out with an ex)?

Is it honesty? Is it all? Is it all right to have secrets? Does he care if you pick his mobile up and watch or hear his voice mails? His phone, what about?

It doesn't matter whether I'm through his phone contact, voice mails or emails, and it doesn't matter if I'm going through my relationship. I only have his and my passwords—because we keep them in one place. I've got his. Such transparency creates confidence.

Is your life entirely interwoven with each other?

You share both bank accounts, for example, or do you have separate accounts and he?

Some of them may be in the future—as I said previously, there are several different stages, but it's important to know what you want in not only the present stage, but also the next stage, so that when you get there you don't get surprised.

You may be on the same page as he was at first, but once you have two children, it is not time to find out that your commitment is strong or not because now the expectations are very different.

You might also start to look for signals that you are committed to when you're in this serious moment of a new relationship, when you know that you are in love and ready for commitments. It's really exciting to go from casual to dedicated couples but it isn't always easy to hop into a new relationship sometimes.

All people take time and do things, especially important things like committing themselves to someone seriously. People are different. Certainly, as soon as we met my husband and I married pretty, but we're not the norm, exactly.

If you're looking for signs to commit your partner, even though you didn't need to talk about it yet, don't seek more. Here are some subtle signs showing that they have happily committed themselves to you:

1. A sure sign that the person with whom you are committed is that they really hear when you're talking— not just pretending that you listen, but actually paying careful attention to what you say.

You will know that your significant other person is listening to you when you ask about that big work project that you mentioned or when they surprise you with tickets to the show that you chatted about the other night. When you realize how much the person you love values what you say, you'll be subtle and sweet.

My husband remembers things that I don't even remember, and he's always aware of how close he listens to me. He always knows how I feel. So if you really care about your partner's thoughts, they will probably commit themselves to you and to him for good. Commitment this is what I believe: Commitment is what you have chosen each other and your significant other. More importantly, it is to support and respect each other's vision. It can require sacrifices and a willingness to take a different view from your own. It also includes each of you, as if you were one, pledging to care for each other as you do for yourself.

Every partner must also choose itself as an undertaking. Nobody can pressure you to do something, I don't believe. Certainly, you can try, but ultimately, every person's own free will must have a true engagement from the heart.

Commitment concerns feelings, ideas and, perhaps most importantly, actions.

Basically, actions speak more clearly than words. He may think a little of you, and he has immense feelings for you, but they don't translate into acts—but this scenario is extremely unlikely. The truth is he would call, write, send you flowers and take you to his favorite restaurant or something if he's thinking of you. This is the point. This is the point. Both partners must be there to win it. It takes two to make the world go around. And I should also like to say that the expectations and definitions that an engagement signifies both must be equal.

The problem is that many of us have such a vague idea of what commitment really means we can't seem to find it or get it from our guy. It's no wonder. We consider it as a kind of untold "bond"— whether it was a combination of all three, spiritual, emotional, physical or certain.

When we see it, we think we're going to know, but that is not a very robust plan, really.

A much better plan is to decide in advance what your contribution would entail. What does your future life, your commitment to the future look like every day?

In the end, you're the only person who can tell us what type of engagement you really want. Tell them then—and write them down. Think about it, really.

Defines it to yourself to the extent that your view of commitment and what it looks like through each of the stages is crystal-clear in mind. It all makes a difference in the world to know what it is for you.

The difference between doing what you need and what you are unable to do.

 You are a part of his life.

A person who is committed to you, rather than just a hookup, will see you as a true partner. They will probably come to you for help and even ask for your advice and your opinions.

One of my husband's favorites is that he enjoys asking for my opinion on issues. It could be the little subject that he should add, or the biggest ingredient, as I think of a potential job, at the dinner he is cooking. However, he always asks me. If you are uncertain about the level of commitment to you of your partner and make sure that they receive your advice or opinion wherever possible, don't worry, as they are certainly there for the time being.

You're still physically fascinated by someone who is truly dedicated to you, you don't hesitate anywhere—at home, in the gym, or on a date. You and the rest of the world will want you to know how you feel.

Even when they're with you and when they learn you'd like to commit yourself, they won't be able to keep away from you even if you're with someone who doesn't have a natural propensity for physical affection or who were really affectionate and romantic in their previous relationship.

My husband is usually far more affectionate emotionally than I am, but if we touch, I find that I love him in a way I never had in any previous relationship. I like to kiss it at home, I like to cuddle it. And it also makes me glad when we're out to always have a hand or really sit closely on him.

5. He mentions commitment before you happily: anyone who's committed to you already won't be entirely new to the idea of commitment.

That doesn't necessarily mean that they've had to be in the long term, but it does also mean you thought about it, you've got an idea of what it is, and it's something you could like to share with you. Someone who wants to engage may speak about the relationship between his or her parents or talk about how, for example, he or she wants a committed partner one day.

If a person doesn't want to engage in a relationship, he does not usually talk about a commitment as if it is a good thing. I didn't really know about marriage until I met my husband, so I never claimed to be. I always wanted to be free. I was always straight. That said, I began to think and speak how good the idea of an undertaking would be when I met him.

You would likely seek that with you if you hear the other one speak about how wonderful they think a long-lasting, dedicated love is.

Many times, when engagement is on the horizon in a relationship, it is clear. But you've got to dig a little other times. But if your partner does any of the things on this list, whether he has said or not, they are committed to you.

Signs that confirm that you two are in a committed relationship

So if your relationship is a serious one, you want to know. Nowadays, it is not enough to assume that your exclusiveness is confirmed by traditional labelling of "boyfriend," "girlfriend," or even "partner." Besides the more evident actions to live and become involved, there are things that never change and there is a strong chance of you being engaged if your relationship has one or more of the following 11 characteristics.

1. One of the very first signs of engagement is that two people spend a great deal of time together. You spend significant time together. Apart from normal working hours and all that you could do in one day, there is generally no time to spare. Since time is one of the few commodities we cannot find back, it is a good sign that you and your important other choose regularly to make time for each other.

2. I had a friend who told me she was in a committed relationship on the day she found herself in a shop with more items in her shopping cart for her partner than for herself— and they were not living in a coexistence. You include everyone else in your ordinary shopping. These activities can be small and evidently meaningless or as lavish as the purchasing of matching gems. Regardless of the purchase, you're probably in a committed relationship if you remember each other to the point where you consider them in your ordinary purchase.

3. When you give somebody a key to your house, don't you remember a Key? Oh, I don't do that either.

It is so emblematic that entire film scenes and magazine articles have been devoted to this rite of committing relationship. If you have one or both keys to the house of the other, you're in it! How many people have your place keys, I mean? There aren't many chances but it's a good sign that you're in a commitment when you do and they aren't your parents.

4. In this era of media chaos it is no surprise that the public announcement of some form of Social Media is one of the first signs of commitment. You've seen them, the amazing and renowned selfie of the pair, the hearty note to see and the hashtags like "I and my son." These public displays are usually quite an excellent indicator of the fact that things are going well. Such shows can only mean "We are serious and we all want to hear about it."

5. Together I think it is fair to say that a major contract between you and your booth is signposted to a major contract (other than a marriage) with someone like buying an item or a car. The reason contracts are so big is that they are often much harder to get out, so most people take care when signing the pointed line and expect to commit for a long time.

6. You holiday together usually take several days and can take a few weeks, so if you go along with your business you will want to make sure that you like them. You are also creating life-long memories. In general, people who spend a vacation together enjoy not just one another's company but also remember it together, so it is a good sign that you and your love are truly committed if you take a holiday together.

7. You think about body functions you're probably not talking around the dinner table about your groin injury or your irritable bowel syndrome. Such talks are usually reserved for health and sometimes amusing cases. But you probably are more than casual friends if you find that you can talk to your lover about intimate functions. This is particularly true if you find that typically private and individual conversations are commonplace between you two.

8. The fact that you and your dear one talk of how to spend hours together is significant if you consider that the average life expectancy is 70 to 80 years old and a third of the time that is spent sleeping. You can take decisions alone if you are alone based on your wishes. However, what the other person wants to do and where he / she sees him / her in a committed relationship matters. There's a good chance you'll have a long-term relationship if you and your partner come up with plans together.

Become Mentally Stronger for continuing reading the article!

Get a FREE Life hack Guide to learn mentally strong and take responsibility for life!

Strengthen up to continue reading article § 9. Scroll down to the table. The number of passwords and pin numbers that any of us has, the number of passwords and pin numbers could mark the end of the few things that we have full control over. Thus, it is not lightly or casually to decide to share this extremely private information. Although experts agree that password-sharing will reinforce ties, this is a sign of participation because it demonstrates absolute trust. So it's still best practice to keep your passwords and PINs secret, unless you're in a committed relationship.

Ten. Another part of being a good citizen of the world takes care of other people, which may mean sometimes going out of your way. But when you leave your path to your wife, it's less work and more we do, you have a keeper and certainly you are committed to it. For example, taking a lunch break for them, reorganizing your plans to travel to ensure you get the time to join you, or giving in your car to make sure you get to the meeting on a timely basis (and, of course, vice versa). Something less and there is no guarantee that you are a committed relationship.

Eleven. Would your partner give up their favorite sweet food bar due to your allergy to the peanut (no kissing for yourself) or traded in your vegetarian pizza in that meat-lover's? You should rest assured that they are no longer committed when they start changing their habits and actions based on your beliefs, conditions and circumstances. Who's doing that, I mean?

It is up to all men, as in all relationships, to express affection, respect and trust regardless of how long they last. However, if you have the characteristics of one of the above 11, congratulations, you are engaged.

This is how a committed relationship appears to be

Are you happy, but you don't know if your partner is fully engaged? Or are you the one who your partner asks about your marriage commitment? We feel safe and secure when two people are involved. Things can feel rocky in the early stages of a new relationship. You know where you stand, neither of you do. You like the person, but if they love you, you don't know.

This can lead to insecurity, jealousy and confidence problems. Even if they say they are loyal to you, how do you know that not only do they say it? This is where you can also help to make your mind relaxed if your eyes are open for signs of commitment.

The little things are the big things in a bond, and the longer you are with someone, the more you become obvious. This could be to cook someone a meal, pick them up and surprise them with their favorite candy bar or even give them a little foot massage after a long day. It's a sign they're loyal to you that you're doing these little things for somebody and they recognize and appreciate them. And if you reciprocate these little gestures, it's also a big sign. A friendship is all about what you can and cannot get from the other person. This ensures that you both abandon your way to care for each other and look after each other. It also requires negotiation and sacrifice to meet the needs of each other. Everything less than that, and you are not fully engaged.

The plans and actions that focus around them are made by individuals. But there are two men to think about when you're in a relationship. You both matter, and it is just as important what the other person wants to do in the future as what you want. And, when you prepare together, or talk about marriage or children, it is a powerful indication that you have committed for a long time. Together planning a holiday is also an excellent mark of commitment, since it involves constantly spending with someone at least a week, usually months in advance. You make memories for a holiday that ends forever–and you won't just want anyone to do that, would you? Both of you are in.

You are both within a committed relationship. You work as a team, and each time you are together you express your love for each other. That may mean verbally or physically, or in small gestures as we spoke about.

It means thinking about how you can bring joy to this person and what you can do to develop as a couple and strengthen your relationship consistently. Even if you're not, you're ready to try and understand each other.

You're not always going to agree, and you have to expect that. It's crucial that both the partners and their needs and points of view are ready to understand from where they came from. You must suppress the ego in order to achieve this and come from a place of pure love.

Even if you don't understand, it's better to be there and listen rather than shut down or try to change the feeling. You met their parents. You met their friends.

You will have liked to get together with each other, as families are usually a large portion of every person's life. It's often difficult to meet our partner's parents; but it's because we know how much it means to them, and we love and respect our partner. This is an undertaking.

You can talk easily to each other easily.

If you can speak openly, frankly and in a comfortable silence to each other, about everything under the sun, it is a great sign that you really like one another, and feel as close as possible to share everything in your mind.

Perhaps when you chat about random nothingness you'll find hours spent, because you lose yourself at that moment. This is a great sign. This is a great sign.

You are asking for advice from each other.

The more feedback you get from your friend, the more your opinion appreciates and you feel comfortable with it. This is a message that you are included when deciding your life, which is a big deal and shows that you and partnership are committed to it.

If these signs appear in your relationship, your partner is very likely to commit himself to you and see you in the future.

Chapter 7:

Ways to Make Your Relationship Strong

It's exciting and challenging to be in a relationship. You will experience lower and higher as a couple. But, if you make continuous efforts, sacrifice and various ways to demonstrate just how genuine and loyal you are with each other you will remain strong and can strengthen even your marriage. However, to make a relationship work, you do not always have to do something big.

There are simple things you can do to improve the relationship.

The Simplest Things

Talk about your day.

Talk to your partner whether you have a good day or a bad day. What keeps you close even if you don't see each other daily is the extent of communication.

2. Give congratulations to your friend.

Tell your partner how good it looks to him / her for his new haircut or dress. Show him / her congratulations so he / she is special to you for making your partner feel.

3. Call your partner things you love.

In addition to congratulating your partner, name at least five things about your partner you love. This is how much he / she loves you.

4. Live together. Drink and eat together.

Regardless of how busy you are, make sure you spend time eating together. A few who eat together remain together.

5. Be thankful.

You may also be used to seeing your partner take extra care of you, but you should appreciate the efforts, small or large, of your partner.

6. Share a good laugh. Share a good laugh.

Bring some jokes on each other. Share the amusing story of your childhood. To reveal a lasting relationship with one another is secret.

7. Do stupid stuff together.

Doing stupid things together can spice up your relationship, so do not hesitate to reveal this mad yet enchanting side.

8. Tell the words of sorcery.

Though the words appear to be overused, don't forget to show love. Tell your friend "I love you," and mean it, of course.

9. Feed your friend. Cook for your partner.

Cook up the food that's full of love and passion for your partner.

10. Let the notes be sweet.

On her lunchbox, place the notes. Say that every day you love him / her. Smooth notes are a smile on the face of your partner.

11. Tell him / her that for him / her you are always there.

Knowing that your partner has his or her back will boost your partner's trust, so you've always been there for him or her.

12. Show him/her everything.

Make your partner accessible to you. Listen to him, listen to him. Listen to him. Weep with him. Weep with him. Weep with him. Just be there for it.

13. 13. Just speak your mind. Speak your mind.

Talk about whether you're upset about something or find something wrong in the relationship. To solve a question of relationships starts by making us aware of a problem.

14. Lift and build up each other.

If you talk to your friend, choose your terms. So avoid additional misunderstandings, be proactive.

15. Talk to one another. Listen to each other.

While you always have the opportunity to voice your concerns, take the time to hear your partner understanding his / her side.

16. Commitment.

A compromise is one way to resolve relationship problems. Talk to each other about what you can do. Consider a spotlight.

17. Say sorry, sorry. Say sorry.

While it's difficult to put aside your pride, if you know you are the one who is fault, learn these words.

18. Fix ASAP problems.

Without you two, don't let a day pass without fixing the problem. It will improve your friendship if it becomes your habit.

19. Be yourself honest.

Often it is neglected, but you must remain honest to yourself so that your partner will be easier to remain honest.

20. Be frank with your partner

When he / she shouldn't be praised, don't praise your partner. Say what you think are mistakes to him / her. Be honest, it's right because it's right.

21. Be faithful and loyal.

Confidence and loyalty go together. Be loyal to your partner and loyal to you so that he / she deserves your confidence.

22. Trust yourself. Believe yourself.

This may not be easy for others, but you just have to believe and trust that you can trust your partner.

23 Trust the words of your partner.

You believe in what your partner says to you. Trust your partner. Doubt only if this is explicitly justified.

24. Confide each other in your love.

Know your affection is greater than any other tentation for one another. Therefore, trust in the love of yours.

25. Don't be too jealous.

You can feel too jealous that you don't trust your partner. Don't be jealous of small, unfair stuff therefore.

26. Do not be suspicious.

Perhaps not getting paranoid would be as easy. However, if you trust your partner enough, you do not need to develop paranoia.

27. Do not be possessive.

Make sure the relationship doesn't stifle your partner. Allow it to do the things it wants to strengthen the relationship.

28. Just keep your promises, always keep your promises.

You say promises must be broken, but you must keep your promises small or big, as a partner and an individual.

29. Enhance the dreams of each other.

You can have an idea of how you would be like lifelong partners if you support each other's dreams. Your relationship is actually strengthened.

30. Be there at the biggest events.

Don't forget birthdays, birthdays, promotions... Your presence means your partner a great deal.

31. Be the number one fan of your partner.

Praise your partner no matter how small or large she's done. He / she's definitely going to enjoy it.

32. Celebrate the success of one another.

Have a luxuriant snack. Get a beer. Get a drink. Celebrate together your success. As friends rejoice.

33. Be proud of him / her.

Tell your partner that you are proud of him. He / she'd love you to hear it.

34. Explain it to others.

Your partner may feel embarrassed about it, but it will surely make your heart melt, if you show the world how proud you are of him.

35. Be there in times of darkness.

Right now, your friend may be upset. Be the one he / she needs the most.

28. Let go of your partner.

If he or she is too stressed at work, leave your partner out. He / she needs somebody to hear him / her and him / she wants somebody to be you.

36. Provide advice bits.

If your partner has something to do, don't hesitate to suggest. That's how much you're interested in him / her.

37. Be a true friend and partner.

Being his / her best friend, not only a partner. The basis of your relationship will definitely be improved.

OUR DIFFERENCE AND DEALLING 39. Follow the dreams of each other.

You might have something different, and its okay. Follow the dreams of each other while maintaining a strong connection.

38. Comply with your differences.

You may have different personalities, but it's important to respect the differences of each other.

39. Hear the important points of your friend.

You may have different preferences in items, but if you listen to and acknowledge the sensitive points of your partner, it's not a problem.

40. Comply with your differences.

You may be special, but the trick is to accept the differences of each other.

41. Listen to the important points of your friend.

You may have different preferences, but it will not be an issue if you listen and consider the important points of your partner.

42. Respect the values and principles of your partner.

You are expected to have differences in values and principles. It is not necessary that we trust each other in your values. Once, appreciation is the key word.

43. Place yourself in the shoe of your friend.

To order to understand the behaviors and decisions of your partner quickly, put yourself in the shoe of your partner.

44. Polite each other. Be polite.

Learn to be mutually cautious. Allow time to grow and give each other relationship.

45. Accept the imperfections of each other.

Know he / she is your perfect partner. Download the defects of each other.

46. Support one another to change.

You are a team, so support each other to develop their skills.

ON QUALITY TIME ON SPENDING

47. Make one of your priorities for your partner.

And make him / her a priority, because it deserves that, because he / she is your friend.

48. Don't think about your moments of cuddling.

Enough cuddling time. It doesn't always lead to sex, but keep in mind that physical contact is an essential love language.

49. Watch Binge together. Binge watch.

Please take a look at your favorite series at binge time. When you are watching the shows you will certainly share laughter, fear and anger.

50. Have a home dinner.

You don't have to go out all you need to do is spend good time. Settle in your home for an intimate dinner and have a pleasure.

51. Go jointly to museums.

Are you a couple's artsy type? Go to museums, enjoy the beauty of art and together create more wonderful memories.

52. Go jointly to the gym.

To go to the fitness center together means to stay healthy and share great times. Encourage one another to stay in form.

53. Cook together. Eat together.

While you can go to a wonderful restaurant, cook at home and enjoy a good moment of interaction. Cook the pasta you want. It would certainly be fun to buy even the ingredients.

54. Take an animal.

While it is caring, the two will develop a strong and entirely different relationship through adoption of a pet.

55. Function for volunteers.

Be successful through voluntary work. You make a difference not only in a strong relationship, but in the universe.

56. Speak under the sun about something.

You can only talk about random things in one way to strengthen your relationship. You will probably learn a lot from each other and explore it.

57. Surprise your partner at a time.

Never forget to take some time in the littlest things to impress your friend. The spark remains alive.

58. Offer a massage to him / her.

Give a massage to your partner after a tiring day on the job. He / she certainly will look forward to it.

59. Show how beautiful she is. How wonderful.

Your partner will know what he / she is drawn to. No matter how long you spent together, never fail to say that your partner is so amazing. 60. Kiss very much. Kiss more.

She kisses on the front, on her lips kiss, on her neck kiss. Kiss a great deal to show you each other that level of affection.

60. Maintain the intimate stuff.

As mentioned, it is important to have physical contact so that this should become a healthy part of the relationship.

61. Work together. Fly together.

Life can become dangerous, so sometimes take a break. Work together. Fly together. Discover together new places. Making together more lovely memories.

62. Try a sport together. Do it together.

Whether or not its extreme sport, do something fun to keep things interesting?

63. Try a new game. Try a different game.

Try to play together, whether it's a board game or a video game. This is another way for you to connect.

64. Interest in the hobbies of each other.

Try to show your partner a lot of interest in stuff. That's what the partner appreciates.

65. Every day, find out about one another.

Regardless of how long you have been together, you can never know something every day.

66. Together you will learn a new skill.

Whether it's new language learning or cooking, try together to learn new skills. Surely you will have to think about something different.

67. Attempt (intimately) new things.

You can study things, intimacy included. Try creating more. Try to be more intriguing.

68. Just have me time. Have me time.

If you are together every second of the day, your relationship can become toxic. You're still a unique person, and you'll take some time. So don't forget to spend time and time on your own.

69. Try to do things of each other.

One way to strengthen a relationship is to let each other continue to do the things you love, so keep on hobbying.

70. Work alone. Fly alone.

You have to be alone even while it's fun to fly with your friend. Try to travel alone for the break you need.

71. Spend time with friends. Spend time with friends.

To keep things balanced, strengthen your relationship with your partner and friends.

72. Take your own groom.

Allow yourself a nice makeover from time to time. Even if you've got a partner you need that.

73. Love yourself. Love yourself.

Don't forget to love yourself as it gives you the ability to love more.

74. Be yourself. Be you yourself.

It is just yourself that is a secret of a strong relation. Your partner is going to love you.

75. Improve the shortcomings.

To deserve your partner, you don't have to be perfect. Submit the flaws, as if he / she loves you too, he / she will do so.

76. Try to improve yourself.

Do not stop looking for self-improvement when you tolerate your imperfections. It's your own creation.

77. Stay independent. Just stay independent.

Remember that staying independent while you are committed to your partner is a sign that your relationship is healthy and strong.

78. Think before you act. Or you say something.

Make sure you stay fair so that when you compete you will not hurt your partner badly.

79. Lower your voice.-Lower your voice.

Rising the tone is not going to lighten the situation. Stay calm so that you have a clear mind on your relationship.

80. Stress your thoughts.

You're crazy because you care for him. Stress your plans to get your partner to accept them.

81. Study your struggles. Learn.

Remember all the challenges you've earned. Do not make the same errors. Do not make the same mistakes. You can strengthen the basis of your relationship through these struggles.

82. Don't be historic or hysterical.

You can get emotional and ancient when you are at the height of your emotions. Stop it to keep the fighting from escalating.

83. Allow your family connection.

Make the extra milestone by developing a real relationship with the family of your partner. Your companion will be able to see his / her beloved well.

84. Get to meet your family. Get to know your neighbors.

Take an effort to know them, not to question his family. Probably your spouse will appreciate your efforts.

85. Notice the small things.

You might suggest that you too well know your partner. Just make sure you see the little things that make him happy or crazy.

85. If possible, stay up late.

Your spouse must know you are prepared to wait until he / she is safe to return home.

86. Make some small sacrifices.

Do not hesitate to give nothing. If you really love your partner, that isn't a problem.

About planning future.

87. Just talk about it. Discuss about it.

Talk about the future. Talk about the life ahead. You have nothing to do immediately. You can only share your views on the future and potentially draw up plans.

88. Do not feel under pressure. Do not feel under stressed.

Don't necessarily feel the pressure to settle. You should know when a strong relationship is ready or not.

89. Keep your eyes open.

Stay open-minded when considering your future, because your plans will change.

90. Do not make hasty decisions.

Once, the next level of stuff isn't a sprint. Let your relationship build up first before you hit the next step.

91. Change priorities. Set targets.

Jointly define short-and long-term targets. Consult to them, and when it's time to settle it, you will learn.

92. Make your tolerance moderate.

There is a degree of flexibility in a strong relationship. You need such power, because all and everybody has limits.

93. Get to say no. Learn to tell no.

In fact, it's necessary to say no to reduce your resistance. You can't always give and do just things, and your partner has to know that.

94. Stand your ground. Stay firm in every situation.

You must stand your ground once you say no. It's for you both to make a difference in the connection.

95. Tell your reasons. Tell them everything.

You said no because there are explanations for this. Tell your partner these explanations to prevent more disputes.

96. Do not post anything online. Do not publish anything online.

Anything or anyone can discourage you from posting online, but you don't have to post anything online in a happily healthy relationship. Do it for yourself, if you write, not to prove to others.

97. Always talk to your partner before you talk to others.

Talk directly to your partner if you have difficulties in the marriage. Through a friend's mouth, do not let him / her know the problem.

98. Keep your secrets. Protect your secrets.

Your partner shares with you his / her secrets because he / she is comfortable in you. Consider yourself deserving of this trust

99. Celebrate your partner's personality and embrace his/her flaws.

100. Honor your wife. Respect your partner.

It's straightforward: value him as your friend. As a person, respect him / her.

In reality, a roller coaster ride can be in a relationship. It can be very difficult. Nonetheless, the above list shows that you can do something to improve the relationship. You may look easy, but it's your goal, your honesty and your effort. So, couples, stay strong!

Chapter 8:

Ways to regain love relationship

How in a relationship do you recover love? It's hard and long without easy fixes, but you can do something to recover a partner's attention, either as a longtime friend or as a new relationship. This happens to the best of us— there is a moment when something seems to break and you realize that your friendship is now boring and that you have become a shared partnership of intense love. You are happy to be together, but not passionate about love.

Everything is brand new when we begin our relationship, so the feelings you experience fill you with pleasure. It is normal, however, that these feelings begin to dissipate after a certain amount of time. While you still feel something in your life's main squeeze, not all of love involves. So how do you get love back when a relation reaches that stage?

Phase 1: Take a reverse phase to proceed.

Try and remember the days, weeks or even years (if you're very happy) that were like these first few. Ask yourself what you did and how you treated each other differently. Then try to relive these moments together with your boyfriend or husband.

Go back to a nice fancy restaurant on a first day, and perhaps order the same meals that you'd have back then. Get love and enthusiasm back! Just forget about calories and children for one night and save the week! These little things can be important when trying to trigger your mind to remember how you felt about someone and why.

Phase 2: Compromise and adjust!

Compromise: this is a key word I can't emphasize enough. Compromise: Commitment! You usually know at this stage of your relationship if your significant other person is against something or would like to take part in an event in which you don't have an interest. To order to counter this you will have developed a rapid response system: "No, I don't want to do that" or "We will go to the dinner parties, whether or not you like it." Such kinds of stock reactions do not lead to good, happy relationships and can keep the relationship from being loved again. Rather, consider your response to a request from your partner consciously, think about what your partner said and give you a clear and measured answer. With time, ideally, you will learn to compromise those things, and he'll realize it and respond if he wants the relationship to continue and your love to return. Even if you disagree or say no, the fact that you clearly thought about the answer before answering will do the good. And yeah, in fact you might enjoy some of the things you'd never do before!

Phase 3: Build new relationships and have more social life.

You may have to open your horizons in order to regain love so that the man begins to seek attention in his life. You will enjoy your time together a lot more when you spend time alone! Those external desires could be anything you find fascinating or want to try (except of course an affair). If you have kids, meet and spend time with other parents. If you want to be fit, take part in a fitness center and start training your body, not yourself.

Perhaps you had a dream always of spending time painting and other creative hobbies. That's your chance! There is one thing your person will join you in all these activities. These activities are normal. If you do, you can discover a shared love for a hobby or skill, and spend some extra time together. If it doesn't, you're going to start being happy at least, so if you're happier, you're going to get a lot of love back all around you.

Phase 4: Do not play games:

Monopoly or Scrabble, I don't think! The games of the mind and the digs will end. In one of these verbal struggles, you may feel justified, but over time, they will not only wear you out, they will also kill the desire of your companion to be with you. Begin to be straight and not to bat about the bush and to make snide remarks. Mind games can be enjoyable and totally harmless in some cases, like bullying in the bedroom or playing war. In fact, this can contribute to a good connection and remind you healthy why you love each other. But the little arguments that after a while can begin to sink into a relationship do nothing to help you regain the love that you felt when you first met. To do or to say things "to return" will always lead to regret for someone.

Phase Five: Be honest.

Honesty— one word, but probably the key aspect of a relationship, and surely an essential part of the recovery of love that might have gone. At some time in your bonding, I'm sure you were honest when nothing seemed to me to be tabuistic, and you could tell your partner all about yourself. Things change as we evolve, and there are two things.

First, with your significant other, you will feel more comfortable and can talk about things which have embarrassed you before. The other thing, though, is you start to feel awkward telling him any details, for example about a fellow worker hitting you or sexual repression you have experienced.

You just omit things because you don't want to hurt feelings. It may not be big, but all these little lies and dishonesty may cost you a life together. Try to be open with your partner 100 percent instead. You will find one another opening up and fostering respect for one another, and also making it easy for one another to chat and connect.

Phase 6: Trust yourself.

After that, faith is the secret to a lasting relationship of love. With it working together. Loving isn't clear if you don't trust your partner. If we allow this, we are consumed by untrustful thoughts. The restoration of love without confidence will be an uphill struggle so that you can get to work as soon as possible through your insecure feelings. Ask yourself why you lost your faith in your guy once and what you or he could do to get this right once more.

Phase 7: Communication is key.

Just as honesty and trust is one of the key components in the recovery of marriage, and interaction is necessary to reinvigorate the relationship. Discuss the weather, the new American idol and the movie to see, honestly and openly. Ask him how he worked his day, and tell him what yours had been like. Though it seems obvious, how many couples fail to sit and talk to each other is shocking. Small transformations can help you open the doors to what is important to discuss.

Phase 8: Restore the passion.

You had your food and are now sitting, sipping wine on this second first day. You have been out. Don't allow the night and the closeness to end, instead keep your hands, brush your hair off of your face, and usually fuse the man you love. He may have to be motivation, especially if he is inexperienced with it, but if he was a romantic young man once, he still has it in him, he just has to coax it out.

You never know where the night will end when you make that first move! In general, romance is essential to recover love in your relationship. These and the other measures mentioned provide an excellent framework for recovering loved one you don't wish to end in this relationship. Teamwork is important, as with everything, so get your partner into the program. If he doesn't or can't, then it's probably time to look for a new partner who knows more about your love.

Ways to reunite with your lost relationship

Many people dissolve because of differences in the past. You could have misunderstood your sister or your parents feuded. Perhaps you just let a friend go. Sometimes a bitter conflict from the past can prevent the reconciliation of the beloved.

But you can start resolving disputes and misunderstandings with friends or family with some effort.

These are the five main steps for restoring any relationship.

- You should first determine your intent before trying to contact a missing friend or relative. Why should this interaction be made? Here are some of the reasons for your situation:
- You know that life is too short to bear anger.
- You are prepared to forgive.
- You are looking for pardon.
- You admit that you hadn't previously tried to reach out.
- Your viewpoint is to be appreciated.
- Before it's too late, you want to share your feelings.
- You want to recover the lost friendship and are ready to compromise.
- You admit that there is no perfect time, no time like today, to reach another person.
- Humbling yourself when you make it clear that you are more likely to humble yourself and accept the risk of being insecure when you touch a former friend or separated parent.

You must also recognize that peace is not assured. It is uncertain what you are doing. Don't let your life be frozen by fear. You become more fragile because you want to heal without taking action. You have a chance to get what you want by putting yourself on the line. Learn if you're incorrect to admit. The earlier we get embarrassed and admit abuse, the easier we can harmony.

Listen to understanding Communication has no value unless shared hearing is the basis. Take time to hear the other person's views and understand them. Put your thoughts away and really try to appreciate the suffering or misery they still feel. Remove guilt journeys. Defend your position while leading the other person to a trip of guilt will only rekindle the flames which have first burnt the relationship.

Forgiveness Offering Forgiveness in all relationships is a strong gift. If you really want to step beyond the past, you must be willing to offer forgiveness.

You do not accept the other person if you offer forgiveness. You do not allow your differences to rule your soul, mind, and future by offering forgiveness. Please remember that, while you may be prepared to meet your friend or family member, the other person may take time to consider your suggestion and answer. Don't hurry to meet or the partnership may not have time to reconcile completely.

Have realistic expectations: Your desire of regeneration will only lead to loss without realistic expectations. It may be impractical for your friend or family member to proclaim your faults and to beg forgiveness immediately. Their response or lack can't be controlled. You should brace yourself for their response. Your acts and the way you live your lives are yours.

Reconciliation and restoration are powerful if authentic healing is based on them. Regardless of how the state of affairs unfolds, you and the other person need to retain dignity and respect. Go forward and love the people with whom you are every day.

Self-Love and Love Relationship

"Two half-fulfilled individuals do not come together to make a whole, complete life an exceptional love. Two people from around the world connect and improve their already fulfilling and beautiful lives with outstanding love. "~Pia Scade My husband and I recently discussed our relationship.

We both said how much the relationship we loved. We haven't been thinking about the degree to which we love each other, but about the extent to which our relationship is familiar to us.

We give and nurtured it with pleasure. We're happy to receive it. It tests us constantly, but these challenges eventually make us better.

We believe that our friendship strengthens and makes us happy. We don't need it, we don't rely on it, but we definitely want to keep it.

For me, it hasn't always been like that. Everything still started well with past girlfriends, but with time my insecurities were taking over.

I'd lose my sense of myself and get lost in the connection. For fulfillment, joy, affirmation and self-worth, I will come to rely on partnership. Sometimes my other half had a similar battle.

As a result, the positive energy between us was drained. The positive energy. The more we needed it, the toxic it became.

We stick to each other, because we thought we needed each other, but we were resentful and despised the relationship. None of us did anything to nourish our love. It was so horrible that we hung up that someone screamed, and it stopped.

The distinction is self-love, then and now. I have been confused and vulnerable in the past, and I didn't know yet who I was or what I wanted in love and life. My friends experienced similar issues and my interactions will eventually become strained.

I can honestly say that I love myself, and that I am content to be myself after many personal progress and self-realization in a partner who has done the same thing. Self-love now means that I esteem my relationship as well. I'm not like I did in the past relying on it, and it's not taking my personality away. It seems like such a simple concept but it was a great epiphany in our recent conversation when we both came to realize this.

We love each other, we love each other, but even after the rose tinted glazes fall off, we love what we call "us." We think the space between us is perfect, as partners, teammates, friends and friends.

Learning Self-love while in a relationship if you don't have any self-love, it can be difficult to be in a relationship. Insecurity frequently results in tension, and the confrontation often breaks down.

One common advice is that before you even get into a relationship, you have to learn to love yourself.

But what if you're with somebody already? Does it mean that you must part before you find love again, to work yourself? Do you need to satisfy an arbitrary criterion for self-love before qualifying for a relationship?

It certainly helps to have a deep feeling of self-love with each other. I often believe, however, that if you are married, with lack of self-love and insecure, annoying, and negative space between you, things can be improved.

Self-love is a process that is ongoing. You can only click this is not a switch. But pairs that have healthy self-love might have more.

How do you develop self-love if you are connected 1? Preserve the level of space and autonomy.

It is unhealthy that your relationship consumes and loses itself as an individual. It is not safe. Have your own habits, hobbies and family. Take a good time to spend your own time nurturing your soul.

2. Think of your own happiness as a master.

It can't make you happy with your partner. That is the only thing you can do. He or she can increase your own happiness, but it is not their responsibility to make you happy. It is their responsibility. You will drain the space between you if you depend on them for happiness. Ensure that you take your own responsibility.

It is not easy to do and you have to develop this habit over time. This starts with the belief that happiness is an option that ensures that you can achieve happiness on your own. It is hard and difficult, but it is free, because you refuse to let your happiness be determined by your circumstances or others.

The only one who can change is you, to choose happiness means to embrace the truism. You focus on yourself and ensure you fulfill your own needs instead of seeking to change others.

The choice to be present is another way of taking responsibility for your own happiness. You will always wait while you wait for the perfect conditions before you can be happy.

You now choose joy instead of thinking, "I'll be happy if..." You silence past and future feelings, and resolve to be content.

It allows you to do the little things that make you happy. You must take up small moments every day, like sitting with a taste of tea or meditating for 10 minutes. This can help calm your mind, encourage you to be here and enjoy your day to have a moment of happiness.

Working in your baggage from the past can also help make the choice of happiness lighter and more present. However, it's a continuous process for working through past pain and while it's good to do so, you don't need to hold yourself away.

"I'll be glad once I get over my baggage," it doesn't need to be. Right now you can be happy.

3. See what your friend sees in you.

Insecure people are struggling to see something good within themselves and sometimes ignore what their partner sees as beneficial.

Ask your partner what you see and what you care most. This is a great date for couples at night. Write a list and take turns reading twenty things you love each other.

If you do it daily, you're going to take it slowly, internalize it and trust it.

For example, for being too quiet and boring, I used to be critical of myself. But I realized I really appreciated my partner's ability to maintain an even knee in harsh, emotional waters.

My highs are not so high, but my low ones are not so low. I now see this as a sign of strength and something positive that I contribute to the relationship, instead of being boring and dismissive of.

You don't just learn about the other person in a relationship, you even learn about you.

4. When you see your flaws, don't get disheartened.

A friendship on the other hand always holds a mirror of your flaws. You can irritate your partner by the things you have learned to live with.

We've all got our shortcomings. Some issues can be ignored; other items you want to focus on might be others. Let it not get you down or get into the way of self-love either way.

The presence of flaws is a natural part of a connection, not that you are or are unlovable. You're a lousy individual.

5. Excuse yourself for your shortcomings.

This gets in the way of self-love by a rebellion against yourself. In a relationship, it is inevitable that sometimes you say or do things you regret. Don't beat yourself about it. Don't beat yourself.

6. It's an event and not a feeling to remember passion.

Sage minds have always believed that passion, not an emotion, is something to do. Sometimes they say this about loving someone else, but the same applies to loving oneself.

Even when you do not like your relationship, choose to act in a way that you value yourself. Give yourself time to cultivate and fulfill your own needs.

This is best done by planning "my day" every day. This is a time when you put yourself above any other undertakings or individuals. Do basic things. Perform simple activities. For me, it goes to the fitness center, reads the news, and has a quiet dinner. Many people enjoy meditating, doing yoga or reading.

It's about developing a little routine of self-love. One session may not matter, but if you can make it a daily habit, you will get cumulative benefits.

The early riser Brigade won me over, because it is not many obstacles that the morning is the perfect time to schedule it. I have woken up an hour earlier than usual every day during the past year, and therefore I am in constant self-love. In the night, you might like to do it like the wind, but make that a priority, in any case.

—Remember, self-love is vital for a happy relationship, safe and respectful. You pump positive energy into your room when you are comfortable and secure and feel good about yourself.

If you feel that you have a difficult relationship, concentrate on yourself, work on self-love and find things better

Key to finding true love is Self-Love

~Sonya Friedman The moon gleamed brilliantly on that busy summer night in the park. "The way you treat yourself is the norm for others." He'd arranged a meeting to "sort things out." I actually had the confidence to go abroad, little he understood. This is what I did, exactly.

I've been saddened but relieved also. I've been home, finally.

I was missing his affection for the longest time. I wanted his cooperation. I needed his agreement. I wanted to end up happy so much.

What is the reason? When I was with him, I said everything. I felt kind of dignified and free.

I wasn't, however. All my energy I would have given away. I had to feel love for him.

And he knew it, but he did treat me. It was a match for him and all our issues somehow always came back to me. I was vulnerable, nervous, and totally unaffected about who I was and what I really wanted. In an effort to try to please another being, I would have sacrificed all about me.

And I read book by book how I can be more feminine and alluring, so I was not attractive enough, he told me. He told me that I was too relaxed and I was so happy and bubbly out of way. He told me I took too long, so I did other plans, and for a while I disappeared.

He could have said anything to me and I'd have accepted anything. In my bones wasn't there an ounce of autonomy. This is exactly what gave rise to my misery.

For so long, I would let it happen. It wasn't his fault entirely. Our issues had been exacerbated and compounded by my neediness and lack of self-worth. But for a reason that I can't explain, I would finally have had enough of a spark that evening.

I was going to reach my limit of pain. I was entirely done with negative thoughts, fears and disrespect. I've been about letting someone else influence my decisions, feelings, and self-worth.

A little more than I loved him, I had begun to love myself. The cold dark cocoon that I kept in my childhood was a butterfly. It felt new and frightful but it inspired and liberated unbelievably.

A sequence of epiphanies melted my confusion in a moment of clarity: profound love comes from within.

I've decided how I want to act.

Only with love from someone else will I never be satisfied.

I can't expect anyone else to really love me if I don't love myself authentically.

The manner in which I treat myself shows others how I look.

I vowed to start my career that evening, and to be kind, friendly and generous. That's how I wanted to be dealt with. I went away from respecting myself and needing a new beginning. It was my dream to live my life on my terms from that moment on.

It may sound egoistic, but it was completely the other way around. And finally it led me to my dreams ' lifetime friendship.

What is the real effect on relationships of necessity?

I sincerely believe it is absolutely priceless to share the joys and wonders of life with another being who shines the heart. Nothing is like it. There is nothing. It is one of the world's greatest joys and something every human deserves.

But if you are in a relationship with a need to be satisfied by someone else, it's extremely difficult to find that fulfillment.

Being in need, uncertainty and trying to gain your partner's approval and self-worth puts a lot of pressure on them and this is a big turnaround.

It's a timeless task since it comes from within to feel inherently loved and dignified. The friend doesn't.

Two half-full people who come together to make one entire, complete life are not an outstanding love. Two people come together to connect and to improve their wonderful and already full lives. Great love.

An incredible relationship arises when we know who we are and accept the other person for whom we are totally.

So first of all, loving and placing you is not selfish. The beautiful love and life that we all want is important. And let's get something straight— the love tank does not deplete yourselves; in reality it fills up so that we have more to offer.

What is the true look of self-love?

You place your dreams in the focus and strive to do inspiring and enlightening stuff.

It says no to things with which you disapprove or which do not fit with your plans.

It is determined to spend time supporting, encouraging and motivating people to be the best version of you.

He holds your opinions and thoughts and refuses to be swayed to satisfy others.

He's smooth to you and He's good and sweet to you.

It has the courage to experiment with new things you have always wanted.

He takes time out to nourish your mind, body and soul–workout, good food, time alone.

He is your trust and your truth that you honor.

He spends money on stuff that makes you feel wonderful when you invest in your future.

It's daring to assume that the life you imagine can be achieved and created.

He wants you to see the positive and not allow others to bring you down.

It gives you forgiveness and accepts all of your beautiful and not so cool qualities.

How do you build a great relationship with self-love?

We are clear of doubt and endless concern, and so we have confidence in our feelings and choices when we truly love and respect ourselves. It enables us to be brave and true.

We start to live from the heart and play a more caring, children's life version. We forget our self-imposed boundaries and wilder and bigger dreams.

We stop concentrating on negativity and become conscious in and out of our beauty and possibilities. They appreciate the goodness of our lives and open the doors to endless appreciation.

Glory, faith, love, harmony, and positivity begin emanating.

It's magnetic to others and it's like a strong magnet. Your ideal partner will be attracted to you like a fresh bear who wants his first meal out of winter.

And once you meet the unique one, it's easy to love.

It will be natural. It will be human. Without bias or pretense, it will flow freely. It's going to inspire and feed you. Your lives are even richer, joyous and more complex than ever before.

And why have you not taken the time to love you radically a little sooner? And you are going to wonder

Ways to keep your man

He wants to be your hero — let him, therefore. Infidelity in relationships is a big concern. It is important to know why people cheat (and how to keep your guy from doing it to you) whether you are cheating before or to avoid it from ever happening.

Because they no longer love you, most people do not cheat. Men cheat because in their sex life they want more variety.

Some men complain that they are bored. You want your friends to be adored. You want to reaffirm your liberty. You are tired of being deceived.

You want a partner who puts it at the core of your life, and you don't feel like your priority anymore.

Sometimes it is because you speak different languages of love, and some men say it is a biological directive to breed for the species ' survival with as many women as possible. Regardless of the reasons, people have an inherent need that their spouses respect and appreciate. It is most troubling for a man to know that he has somehow deceived his partner. He want to be her hero. He wants her. Here are also ways to hold your man and prevent him from cheating in love with you (and you alone):

1. You are ready to start sex.

People associate sex with convenience. Help the man feel like he is by physically expressing his love.

2. Be open to testing.

It can be easy, and fear of the unknown will keep you from being open to various sexual experiences.

Let your husband seek with you new things. If you do not, somebody else will. If you do not.

I'm not saying you're repulsive in engaging in sexual activity, but let the guy you want experience new things.

3. Don't over accommodate. Don't over accommodate.

A woman can sometimes be too welcoming in a relationship.

Men have a very clear picture of how a girlfriend looks and this is often clearly in comparison to whom he has dated socially. Women are working to be their partner and they lose themselves in this way. One day, their man knows that's what he wanted, but he doesn't know what he wants. Continue your friendship with a good sense of self

4. Do not become too controlled. Do not become toxic.

Often without knowing it, we try to control the other person to do what is best for us when we get into relationships.

We practice destructive relationships such as lamentation, blame, criticism, harassment, threats, punishment and bribing or rewarding for control.

5. Make sure he knows how grateful you are.

Often, when women marry, they get a false sense of safety. Once women are married. All links are voluntary. Remember.

At any time, a person can leave. With the divorce rate in this country, we must remember the value of sustaining, not merely gaining a positive relationship.

6. Let him get time for himself.

Some people cheat because their relationship is hemmed in. Engaging in an affair can give them a sense of freedom in a relationship that they lose.

Without you, let your man have time for himself. Don't try monopolizing the entire time of your guy. Be open to spending time apart, so he doesn't feel free to spend with family, pursue hobbies, etc.

7. Keep your emotions alive.

Whether we are conscious of it or not, women are master of their feelings, without words, to express volumes. We express our partners ' frustration, rage, sorrow and disappointment.

Instead, several men start searching for another companion to idolize the way you used to, as a guide for doing something else. Don't forget that your guy wants to know that he's lighting you— not that he's always dishonest. 8. Consider your friendship a priority.

Also, if a man cheats, the wife has an affair that's not romantic too. It's socially more appropriate.

This adultery takes the form of giving priority over the relationship to something— something. It might be a work, baby, sick relative, charitable organization or anything that places her husband in a lower totem than in the first place. Make your relationship more important than anything else. This is your entire life long friendship. Something else will disappear and if you stick to it, the connection will still be there.

9. Learn the language of his devotion.

When you don't know the five love languages of Dr. Gary Chapman, please read them. It is capable of saving more marriages than marriage advice. Learn and talk regularly to your man's love language. He knows that he's loved and stays true to you. Ten. Find your pattern of partnership.

I don't know how to fight the debate about biology. Many men simply believe that sexual encounters with as many women as possible are hard-wired into their DNA.

Hopefully it won't matter what you do if this is your guy. Seek early in your query about their date background to identify these people.

If this is your man's pattern, he probably won't change only because you love him best. Your best defense against this problem is to begin with to discriminate.

What about him if you read this article and wonder now? What's he going to have to do?

I just want to write a women's article. I see more women in distress because of the unfaithfulness of their fellow than I do people. To you, that's it.

Don't point your finger at your friend if you're upset about your marriage. See the mirror and decide what triggers frustration.

Ask for something other than your man, if you want something else. Good if he gives you what you want! If it doesn't, look for the answer inside yourself.

Consider your guy as he is and adapt to handle your relationship better. And it might be your best choice if he breaks one of your non-negotiable goods.

Some amazingly inspirational love quotes for loving souls

The most thrilling and enjoyable thing can be love.

Live Love. It is the only thing that really matters, but when it calls to you, it can be so heartbreaking.

The best love quotes explain this special emotion in innumerable ways, because one of us can only fully understand what true love is and what it is to say "I love you." If you have been mixed up with love's thousands of imitations, the best educator may sometimes be found reading inspiring love quotes filled with life's lessons and experiences.

Love is the will to extend oneself to foster one's spiritual growth or the spiritual growth of another.

Dr. Scott Peck, "Love is the will to extend oneself to foster one's self or the other's spiritual growth." Love is living without judgment.

The absence of judgment is love.

Dalai Lama: "Love is lack of judgment." Go back to love. Go back to love.

Marianne Williamson's: "Love is what we are born with; Fear is what we have learned here." Before you met, love was present. Finally, somewhere, lovers don't meet. They're all in one another.

Rumi: "They don't meet anywhere, eventually. They're all along in each other". The purpose of love is for the joy of others.

Richard Bach: If they come, they are yours; if they're not, and they were never. "When you love somebody, they'll free you. Love knows no time. Love does not know time."

Jeff Brown: The longest relationships often yield no development, while the shortest of interactions change all. It does not take the heart to look at it."

"To love you don't measure time in time. More than material, love is Love is not only physical .The spirits schedule important meetings long before the bodies touch.

Paulo Coelho: "The souls are planning important meetings long before the bodies look at one another."

"Loving needs the soul to obey. True love leaves no alternative for you.

Caroline Myss: "True love doesn't leave you with a choice." You are going to attract what love you offer.

You show love by offering it to yourself unconditionally. And like this you are attracting others who can love you unconditionally to your life.

Paul Ferrini: "You show love by offering it to yourself without conditions, and like you do, you bring others into your life who will without conditions be capable of loving you." Love of oneself is necessary.

It's not egotistic to love oneself, to care for oneself and to prioritize your happiness. This is necessary.

"It's not egoistic to love yourself, to take care of yourself and to prioritize your happiness.

To be seen by someone absolutely and to be loved anyway — this is a human gift that can limit itself to wonders.

Elizabeth Gilber: "It's a human gift that can verge on a magical one, then to be truly seen and accepted in any event." Loving doesn't imply hopes. Real love begins when nothing in return is planned.

Nhat Hanh: "Love starts, if nothing is anticipated in exchange." Love without reason. Hate without reason.

In every one of us, there is absolutely unconditional love. It belongs to our deep inner being.

Ram Dass: It is not so much an intentional emotion as a being. It isn't' I love you,' either because of that or because, "I love you if you love me." It's not' love for no purpose, love without a substance.'

Love without an object is the very thing that exists in each one of us. Loving brings you attributes. You get the strength to be loved by someone deeply while a person loves you deeply. It gives you strength to be deeply loved by someone when you love another intensely. Love is enough. Love is important.

It is loyalty in good and bad times, it is less than ideal and gives life to human weaknesses. Love is happy with the present; it looks forward to the future, and it does not develop over the past. It is the day and day, and it is the twists and the end of time, it is the time of love. It's love. Love is calm, it's loyalty. Loving is a power that unites.

Love alone is able to unite living creatures so that they can complete and satisfy them, because it alone takes them and joins them in the most profound portion.

Pierre Teilhard de Chardin: Love alone is able to unite living beings so that they are full and fulfilled, for it alone takes them and unites them with the most sublime of them.'-. Love looks the same way.

Antoine de Saint: "Love does not consist in looking one another but in looking one other out in the same direction." Beyond the safety of the body, passion lives.

Treasure the love that you first get. Even after your good health has gone it will stay

OG Mandino:"Treasure your love first and foremost, that your health will survive for a long time"

Love keeps your feeling for yourself. There is never a final chapter, because the legacy continues, as you make loving others the story of your life.

Ophelius: "When you make loving others the life story, there's never a last chapter because the legacy keeps going. You give one person the light, and one or the other person shines the light.

Real love is liberty, and that is what the Creator has granted you — the right to love and choose your own course.

"Real love is liberty, and that's what the Creator gave you, the right to love and to choose a way of your own."-

Rainer Maria: the most difficult task, the final test and evidence, the work to which all the other work is nothing but preparation. Loving is both sides' Life is the state in which another person's happiness is important

Robert A Heinlein: "Love is the state in which another person's happiness is necessary for his own." The hand in hand is love and confidence.

David Viscott Caring and loving is experiencing the sun both ways: "Loving and loving the light, you have a sense of the sun both ways"

Elizabeth Barrett Browning "Whoever loves, believes the impossible. Love is the greatest richness. Who's poor if you're loved?

Oscar Wilde "Who, being loved, is poor?" In one another, love sees the divine. Seeing the face of God is to love another person.

Victor Hugo: "Seeing the face of God is loving another person."

Mother Teresa: You don't have time to love them if you judge people.

H. Brown Jackson: Loving is when the joy of the other person is greater than your own.

Oliver Wendell Holmes: Love is the key that opens the gates of happiness.

Lao Tze: Being deeply loved by someone gives you strength while being deeply loved by someone gives you courage.

Aristotle: Love is a single soul that lives in two bodies.

Brigitte Nicole: If a relationship is right for you, you'll learn. It will improve your life, not make your life more complicated.

Charles Kuralt: Family love and friends ' respect are far more important than wealth and privilege.

Wiz Khalifa: Why can't we think about family when everything we've got is money?

Tupac: Ain't a woman alive who could take the place of my mummies.

Payne Stewart: We've grown up in our family with so much respect.

Dalai Lama: Give wings to those you love to fly, roots to return, and reasons to stay.

Will Smith:10 ways to love: listen, speak, give, pray, answer, share, enjoy, trust, forgive, promise.

Drake Love with your heart, not your eyes.

Anne Hathaway Love is a human experience, not a political statement.

Jimi Hendrix: When the power of love overcomes the love of power the world will know peace.

Sam Keen We come to love not by finding a perfect person, but by learning to see an imperfect person perfectly.

Mark Twain LOVE: The irresistible desire to be irresistibly desired. **Eminem** Love is just a word but you bring it definition.

John Keats Two souls with but a single thought, two hearts that beat as one.

William Shakespeare Love me or hate me, both are in my favor... If you love me, I'll always be in your heart... If you hate me, I'll always be in your mind.

Nicholas Sparks: You are my best friend as well as my lover, and I do not know which side of you I enjoy the most. I treasure each side, just as I have treasured our life together.

Theodor Geisel: You know you're in love when you can't fall asleep because reality is finally better than your dreams.

J Cole A little jealousy in a relationship is healthy. It's always nice to know someone is afraid to lose you.

Leonardo da Vinci: Life without love, is no life at all.

Ed Sheeran: All that you are is all that I'll ever need.

George Sand: There is only one happiness in this life, to love and be loved.

I've been through it all and nothing works better than to have someone you love hold you. – **John Lennon**

Atticus I told her I was lost in this world, and she smiled because she was too. We were all lost somehow but we didn't care, we had in the chaos, found each other.

Christina Perri: You need to love yourself and be yourself one hundred percent before you can actually love someone else.

Louis Lit: Don't let the moment pass. Don't let the people you love walk by you without letting them know how you feel about them, because life slips by, then it's over.

Chapter 9:

Law of Attraction and Love Relationship

You probably heard of the Law of Attraction— or, as many people call it, "the secret." It's an essential element of self-help today and has slowly been watered down, like many common ideas, so much so that no one knows what it means.

Yes, the law of appeal works. You can also apply it completely to your relationship and use it to help you get the type of features you want for a new partner.

The problem is that the law of attraction is always misunderstood. You don't know what it really is or what it actually means, so you often misapply it and then dismiss it when it doesn't work. The problem is they don't do it properly.

Nonetheless, you can't really blame them. All the "the secret" propaganda is easily misunderstood, because it depicts very shallowly what it means. You might end up thinking that if you have no more exposure to the concept, it is the same essentially as wishful thinking or magic. This is not. It is not.

Let's look at what is actually the Law of Attraction, and then we can go through a number of ways to manifest love and all sorts of relationships in your life.

"I'm lonely and lonely, and I think there is none out for me," says the Law of Attraction, "What does the Law of Attraction actually mean to you? I think of how much I want a relationship each day? Should I have no idea of the stuff I have in mind? Why hasn't the Universe been giving me a lover yet? This is not the principle of attraction.

It is no wonder that when you attempt to attract a woman, something like the paragraph described above passes through your mind, then you haven't made a connection. This form of thinking is an absence mentality. Whatever you're thinking about, with such an attitude you won't attract anything.

The Law of Attraction is not wonders. It doesn't when over what you deserve. What is not yet here is not complaining. It doesn't dwell on what you don't have, hopefully it will come.

The law of attraction is about focusing on what you want, not the fact that you want it. Stop wanting. There is a significant distinction. You will be able to look for the best route if you concentrate on what you want. When you concentrate on something, the brain will see a shortage everywhere.

The Law of Attraction means that you put your focus where you want to go. Forget that you haven't already been there. Don't allow your issues to linger in your mind along the way. Hold your eyes on the target as you are there already and go ahead.

It isn't necessary to want it. It is only a way to train your subconscious mind; you have yet to take action to fulfill your intent. The rule of appeal is nothing special. Before your circumstances change you are the one to change. The way is through personal transformation to what you want. If you must learn a completely new style related to people, in order to have the relationship you desire, it will be.

In other words, to obtain something else from the world, you must be another human. That's why most people don't. They want to not change. They want to change. They believe that they can stay the same and somehow have different results.

You can possibly already see how this affects relationships. How this affects relationships how many people in good relations do you see in desperation? What have they concentrated on their own lack, soleness and emptiness? Are others appealing to them?

Perhaps not. Not necessarily.

How about people who radiate a feeling of completeness with confidence? You certainly have met someone who seemed bizarrely content to be alone before, if they were needed, but were never unexpected.

At first it appears unfair, isn't it? But if you look a little closer, you will see that it's just how well the rule was enforced by those people without even knowing it.

When you're Lonely Do you really want something for a long time, and never did it happen? The more you wanted it, the more it seemed to run away from you?

It may have been cash or a relation or another condition of life.

Has it ever happened that when you gave up and your life continued, suddenly it turned out from nowhere?

That is the ability to give up. Sometimes it just leads to focus on lack if something "too hard" is wanted. You get desperate eventually. When you let it go, you instantly get the things you want. "Yeah, I'm all right with or without you!"

This is common in solitary individuals who want relationships badly. You can't take silence out of your head. You're ruminating. The pain can even be seen and driven away by others.

Suddenly, when you relax and remember that you are completely fine alone, someone comes into your lives suddenly.

Firstly, your acceptance is determined by the quality of your relationship. You have to be OK. If you are trying to make a relationship manifest when you are depressed and you have poor self-esteem, it can be a victory, but almost definitely the relationship is not the same. You may drive your partner away or, more likely, unconsciously cause drama or attract a partner that is not good for you.

There are incredibly dependent people who cling like a magnet to desperate loners. Would you like to attract such a person? How to use the rule of love (and not the lacune) the best way to make the relationship with a good partner is to fill up your gap before gazing at the hole of your isolation and hoping that anyone appears. Happy people, autonomous people, after all, are drawn to the same kind.

There are some practical things you can do that will motivate you gradually to become the type of person who can easily attract several different partners: #1: Be grateful for the relationships you have before everything else.

Within our culture this can be difficult, as it is designed for us to think about the wrong things in our lives. We often don't even know that our problems are solved or acknowledged as a fact of life.

Well, your solitude isn't life fact. You can be grateful for the stuff you have either alone or not.

In your life, what relationships do you really enjoy already?

Have you got some friends you're so close to? Have you a family that loves? Do you have a good connection to yourself?

Does somebody see you already romantically, but do you continue to poison the link by asking yourself when it will become a "true" relation? Are your demands and desperation driving the individual away?

Relaxation.

Relax. Look around you. Look around. Look around. Even if it is hard to first see through a lens of soleness, there is always something to be thankful for.

It can even be as simple as going out into nature and revisiting your relationship with the animals and plants that live there.

Love: 7 Ways to Use the Law of Attraction to Find a Relationship the hands of Jorge Vamos more are based on experience and observation, which is updated June 14, 2019. Most men— including himself— have been seen, seduced and hurt by passion.

You probably heard about the law of attraction— or the' secret,' as many people call it,' the Law of attraction. It is nowadays a staple of self-help and has been slowly watered down as many popular concepts are, so that hardly anyone else knows what that means.

Indeed, the Law of Appeal works. You can also extend this to your relationships entirely and use it to help you attract a new partner with the kind of features you want.

The truth is, the law of attraction is not always known. You don't understand what it really is or is, so often you misapply it and then reject it if it doesn't work. The question is they don't do it correctly.

However, you can't really blame them. All the "secret" propaganda is easily misunderstood because it is a very shallow representation of the law of attraction. If you do not get to know the idea better, you will finally think it is practically the same as wonders or magic. This is not. It is not.

Let us look quickly at what is actually the law of attraction, and then we can go through a few ways to show you love in your lives in a variety of different ways.

It takes the right personality to attract the right partnership.

It takes the right personality to attract the right partnership.

"I am lonely and alone, and it seems like there is nothing for me out there. I think about how much I want to be partner every day. Would I not be offered what I think about? Why did the Universe not offer me a lover? The Law of Attraction doesn't work!" Indeed, in fact. "The Law of Attraction does not work." This is not the law of attraction.

It's not surprising that you have not shown a relationship if something like the paragraph above is what goes through your mind when you try to attract a fellow man. These thought is an insufficiency mentality. No matter what you think about, with such a mindset, you won't attract anything.

It is not wishful thinking the law of attraction. It doesn't whine over what you want. What hasn't been here yet, it's not crying. It doesn't rely in the expectation that it eventually arrives, what you don't have.

The law of attraction is everything about concentrate on what you like and not the fact that you want it. Stop Wanting. There's a big difference here. Once you focus on what you want, you will be able to learn the unconscious mind for the best way. When you focus on wanting something, your brain will be missing everywhere.

The Law of Attraction means that you focus on where you want to go. Forget that you haven't already been there. Don't let your issues linger in your mind along the way. Hold your eyes on the target, as you are, and move ahead.

It isn't sufficient to desire it. The law of appeal is not magical; it is just a way to train your subconscious mind; you still need to act to achieve your goal. You must adapt to the conditions. You must change. The path to what you want is by personal transformation. If you need to learn a whole new type of people to have the friendship you want, then that's it.

In other words, to obtain anything different from the universe, you need to be another human. This is why it's wrong for most people. Do not want to change. We don't want to change. You think you can stay the same and somehow achieve various results.

You can already see how these impact relationships relate to relationships. How many desperate people in good relations are you seeing? What did they do to concentrate on their own lack, soul and emptiness? Are other people appealing?

Perhaps not. Not probably.

How about people who radiate a sense of totality with confidence? You have probably met someone who appeared oddly happy if they wanted to be single, but never were without prospects.

At first it seems unreasonable, isn't it? But if you look closer, you will see that the difference is clearly how well the Law has been enforced, not even understood by these men.

To manifest love means first of all to find joy in one's own life.

To love manifests means to first find your own joy in your life.

When you're sad you've ever really, for a long time really wanted something and never did it happen? The more you wanted it, the more it just seemed to have disappeared from you?

Perhaps it was money, or a link or another circumstance in life.

Has it ever happened that as you surrendered it and your life went on, all of a sudden it came from nowhere?

This is the ability to yield. Sometimes it leads to the focusing on lack of something "too hard." You finally get desperate. If you let it go you think,' Bah! I'm all right, or without you!' you get what you want instantly.

This is common for single people who want relationships badly. You cannot remove the solitude from your mind. You're ruminating about it. The pain can even be observed and driven away by others.

Then, when they give up and realize that they're all right to be alone, someone comes abruptly.

Firstly, our acceptance will dictate the quality of your relationship. You need to be ok with yourself. When you are full of desperation and have low self-esteem, if you seek to manifest a relationship, you can indeed succeed but almost inevitably the relationship will be inadequate in itself. You may drive your partner away, drama your relationship unconsciously or - more likely-attract a partner not good for you.

There are foolishly dependent people who cling like a magnet to desperate loners. You want to really attract such a person?

A good strategy to attract better friendships is to thank your mates.

A good strategy to attract better relationships is grateful for your friends.

The best way to have a relationship with a good partner is to make up your void first, instead of looking in the void of your loneliness and hoping that somebody will show up. After all, content, autonomous people are attracted to the same type of people.

There are a few habits you can adopt to slowly turn you to the type of individual who can easily attract several different partners: #1: Be grateful for your relationships, using' code' to find what you want means a sense of gratitude.

This can be very challenging in our culture, since we are scheduled to think about our lives. Often, we cannot even understand that solutions to our problems exist and can only accept them as a fact of life.

Okay, it's not about the isolation. You can be thankful for the things you have, whether alone or not.

What relationships do you really enjoy in your life?

You got some friends you are so loyal to? Have you a family of love? Have you a good connection to yourself?

Is there anybody you see romantically, but continue to empty the link by asking yourself when it will become a "real" relationship? Should you drive people away with desperation and demand?

Relax. Relax. Look around you. Look around you. Look. Even if it's tough to see it first with a prism of soleness, there is always something to be proud for.

There can be even something as simple as going out and revisiting your relationship with the animals and plants living there.

Nature will help you feel more full and self-sufficient and allow you to attract your partner indirectly.

You can feel more truly and autonomously enjoying nature and indirectly help you attract yourself to a partner.

#2: let Go of Judgment Many things close us to the ties are overly judgmental about those who appear throughout our lives. A strict "must have" list of a mile is often a form of self-sabotage for our prospective partner.

The reality is that perhaps you don't know what will please you. Loosen a little. Loosen up. Stop concentrating so hard on perfect things and welcome what happiness comes with. This will send the world a signal to send out more.

#3: Don't Sell Yourself Short Just as it's a fool's errand to expect your partner to fulfill your every whim and desire, you shouldn't settle for something way below reasonable standards just because you think you "can't do better." It doesn't matter how unattractive you think you are; no one deserves a partner who abuses or disrespects them. Beware of the signs of someone who is wrong with you and know when to go run, even if it is alone.

"The Universe" is going to try you that way sometimes. You're getting a bad game and waiting for you to see if you're able to decline politically.

You're going to meet new people actively to try and find a relationship?

Hey, we're going to see how that is going.

Yes, I am too shy. I am too nervous.

No, I'm sure someone's going to turn up if I stay in my room long enough. Isn't the attraction law working like that? I attract people to watch Roseanne re-flow and Doritos eat??

#4: Forget the Disney Ending; make your own story It doesn't mean that the relationship will be perfect or permanent. Remember, in a given moment, you'll attract someone who matches you. The relationship may no longer be compatible if you or your partner changes. We are sometimes meant to learn from a relationship, and then start when we are finished.

That's okay and it's not a mistake. Existence is only. Let go of the necessity to live "ever after happily." This is just cultural programs which can ironically interfere with true happiness.

Have your own story instead. What do you want to be in this relationship? Picture it in your own head as vividly as you can. If you can do so in as much depth as you can without thinking inadequate.

#5: Using imagination Make it as true to your mind if you visualize your friend. Imagine yourself going up and starting a conversation with this person. Do it many times in your mind so that you are ready when the time comes to communicate.

Not only is this helping you to feel more confident, but also to look for opportunities. Once you are set, do not be shy! #6: send out your Mating call! Send the world your intention. Tell everyone you know you're looking for a partner.

Remember to not send this message in a critical manner, or it could fire back. Be assured, identify your needs and invite new people happily into your life.

You will have trouble finding one if you are too shy to admit that you are looking for a relationship. Consider as plain as you can what you want.

#7: Create a good life, then welcome others into it, and if you live a life you enjoy, you will inevitably be drawn into droves by men. Someone who actually feels the joy to be alive every day is so rare that people's curiosity will be sparked by this. It will also cater to a good partner.

So one of the best strategies in your life to manifest love is to build the foundation first. Make a life for yourself and see how it flows into the right people.

Nonetheless, be careful here. "Right life" does not mean "a life I believe would get me a partner." Most people are forced into a position that they despise to raise money to attract a marriage partner. This often leads to a miserable relationship.

Create the right life for you and become imaginative. Then you'll probably find the right mates.

Finally, let us have a short word on how a love can be manifested with a particular person.

Don't. Don't do it. Don't do it.

Can a relationship with a certain person be manifested? In theory, yes. Yes. Though, if you even want to do this, usually you have an attitude of scarcity and so it never works.

People who use the Law of Attraction properly to show love are open to anybody who matches well. If you focus too much on one person, then you reject the left and right who can give you the same happiness and joy as you hang up.

This is hopelessness. It doesn't only work to manifest your desires, it will possibly also kill the other guy.

It is probably best to let go of the necessity to be with them if you really want to attract a certain person. Dating other people will make you more attractive, and you could end up together.

Obviously, you can always try the direct method of attraction: ask them, if you like a certain person and believe that the Creator is the one who sent you!

The law of attraction does not mean wanting, as you can see, it's about having. Conclusions

What do you love already in your life? Enjoy and expand it!

How do you have a friendship with yourself? Improve it and in your life you'll see other persons.

Concentrate on your own happiness and let the rest of the things follow you ultimately falling in place.

Let your marriage feel new again, and get your love life back to sparks. This subliminal course will allow you to relax and escape the repetitive movements of your relationship. Learn to be casual and enjoy all the big things the other important person brings to you. Experience the rejuvenation of your love life!

Subliminal and Love Relationship

The subliminal course consists of the calming sounds of the Oyster River in Brittany Columbia, a top person, motivating expert, clinical hypnotherapeutic with over ten years of experience working on INeedMotivation.com and supporting tons of thousands of people who are registered, certified and knowledgeable. Advanced Subliminal. The subliminal course spark provides the same degree of strong, motivating suggestions as our hypnotherapy courses. The way subliminal courses are developed is key in the efficiency of these courses. To build our subliminal courses, we use the highest quality of technology and equipment. At specific times, our strong suggestions can be "set up" into music at the correct decibel level to be hesitant to listen, while at the same time being the main thing the subconscious can consume. This creates a perfect atmosphere in which the user can either relax and focus on these courses or play it in the background while doing something else. Establish relationships that are safe. Listen to your friend and accept it. Discover and apply the secret to productive partnerships. Build a future for which you hope!

The subliminal program of hypnosis works at three different levels–positive statements will be spoken in your deepest state of open relaxation and low-binaural beats, which with your subconscious mind are almost imperceptible to the human ear working, to support positive statements for successful relationship instruments. Those three components coupled with seven separate calming sounds of nature form the triad of positive changes that will propel you to a better future.

Successful relationship Affirms in this program are: I always love and appreciate my partner. I am a great friend and I always have seen how good of my relationship. I am a great listener and I am committed to working in relationships. I trust and believe that I always give and receive love. You can listen to the whole program or only pick specific sounds you like most-the positive statements will still be useful to modify.

Let your marriage feel new again, and get your love life back to sparks. This subliminal course will allow you to relax and escape the repetitive movements of your relationship. Learn to be casual and enjoy all the big things the other important person brings to you. Experience the rejuvenation of your love life!

The subliminal course consists of the calming sounds of the Oyster River in Brittany Columbia, a top person, motivating expert, clinical hypnotherapeutic with over ten years of experience working on INeedMotivation.com and supporting tons of thousands of people who are registered, certified and knowledgeable. Advanced Subliminal The subliminal course spark provides the same degree of strong, motivating suggestions as our hypnotherapy courses. The way subliminal courses are developed is key in the efficiency of these courses. To build our subliminal courses, we use the highest quality of technology and equipment. At specific times, our strong suggestions can be "set up" into music at the correct decibel level to be hesitant to listen, while at the same time being the main thing the subconscious can consume. This creates a perfect atmosphere in which the user can either relax and focus on these courses or play it in the background while doing something else. Establish relationships that are safe. Listen to your friend and accept it. Discover and apply the secret to productive partnerships. Build a future for which you hope!

This subliminal program of hypnosis works at three different levels—positive statements will be spoken in your deepest state of open relaxation and low-binaural beats, which with your subconscious mind are almost imperceptible to the human ear working, to support positive statements for successful relationship instruments. Those three components coupled with seven separate calming sounds of nature form the triad of positive changes that will propel you to a better future.

Successful relationship Affirms in this program are: I always love and appreciate my partner. I am a great friend and I always have seen how good of my relationship. I am a great listener and I am committed to working in relationships. I trust and believe that I always give and receive love. You can listen to the whole program or only pick specific sounds you like most-the positive statements will still be useful to modify.

Conclusion

The book has discussed about what love is, how a person feels in love, the changes that take place in his or her life and how he evolves as a greater human being. Relationships are hard to build and even harder to maintain. One has to bring about a lot of changes in one's personality and thought process to keep the people and bonding intact. Adjustment, compromise, acceptance, empathy and respect empower each and every love relationship.

People should also analyze their relationship and its strengths and weaknesses. This enables them to figure out how their future will be with the person they are in love with. Some characteristics are obvious signs of a healthy and committed relationship. Once you realize that your partner is fair, sincere and good enough for you, let him be your hero in every aspect of life.

Furthermore, if you feel like losing the bond in your relationship, always stay positive, fill your heart with self-love, and propagate the idea of self-worth over settling for less or chasing your love with no self-respect intact. Practice Law of attraction, manifest your love life through law of attraction and subliminal. Always remember that what you give out, universe returns that to you with greater magnitude. Therefore staying positive and focused is the key.

References

1. Ways to keep your relationship strong retrieved from **https://daringtolivefully.com/keep-your-relationship-strong**

2. Ways to regain your love retrieved from https://www.everydayhealth.com/healthy-living/8-ways-regain-love-relationship/

3. Five Steps to reunite a lost love relationship retrieved from **https://centerstone.org/our-resources/health-wellness/5-steps-to-reunite-a-lost-relationship/**

4. 30 Inspirational Love Quotes for People Who Love From the Deepest Parts of their Soul retrieved from **https://www.yourtango.com/experts/carolyn-hidalgo/inspirational-love-quotes-deep-soul**

5. Tips to make your relationship stronger retrieved from**https://inspiringtips.com/things-to-do-to-make-your-relationship-stronger/**

6. Self-love is key to finding true love retrieved from **https://tinybuddha.com/blog/why-self-love-is-the-key-to-finding-true-love/**

7. Law of attraction and love relationship retrieved from **https://pairedlife.com/dating/How-to-Manifest-Love-7-Ways-to-Use-the-Law-of-Attraction-to-Find-a-Relationship**

8. How to Develop Self-Love and Why This Will Strengthen Your Relationship retrieved from **https://tinybuddha.com/blog/strong-relationships-stem-self-love-develop/**

Printed in Great Britain
by Amazon